THE LEADERSHIP OPERATING SYSTEM

A PLAYBOOK FOR ALIGNING TEAMS, ACCELERATING GROWTH, AND DOMINATING MARKETS

JÜRGEN DAUK

THE LEADERSHIP OPERATING SYSTEM

A Playbook for Aligning Teams, Accelerating Growth, & Dominating Markets

Published by Jürgen Dauk

Hamburg, Germany

ISBN: 978-3-9828102-3-2 (paperback)

ISBN: 978-3-9828102-1-8 (hardcover)

ISBN: 978-3-9828102-2-5 (eBook)

BUSINESS & ECONOMICS / Leadership

www.theleadership-os.com

TRADEMARKS

To Silke:

You are the love of my life. What a gift to travel this life journey together with you.

To Ben, Tom and Jim:

Could not imagine a life without you boys. I am so proud of each one of you and love seeing you grow. You are the best kids I could wish for. Love you.

To Karim

Thanks for taking the time out of your busy life to write my foreword. This really means a lot to me.

I also would like to thank the people that supported me with this book. Polly, Bobby, Amanda and Zachariah, without you this book wouldn't exist. Amine, Antonio, Ben, Emanuel, Guy, Jens, Konrad, Kurt, Markus, Mark, Tina and Thorsten, thank you for helping me launch this book. Abdul, thanks for your help, patience and great designs.

To D.F.M.

Grateful for having you in my life.
T.S.O.R.P.

Table of Contents

Disclaimer

The content of this book is based on the author's experience and research and is intended for informational purposes only. Every organization is unique, and the methodologies, frameworks, and strategies presented should be evaluated and adapted to your specific context. This book does not constitute professional consulting, legal, financial, or tax advice. Results may vary, and the author makes no guarantees regarding outcomes from applying the principles in this book. Readers are encouraged to seek appropriate professional guidance before making significant business decisions. All examples and case studies have been modified to protect confidentiality. The author and publisher disclaim any liability arising from the use or misuse of this information.

Foreword

Let me be honest with you: I don't write forewords. Not usually, anyway.

When someone asks me to endorse their business book, my first instinct is to politely decline and suggest they find someone with more patience for corporate platitudes. After all, the business book world is already drowning in recycled frameworks, buzzword bingo, and "revolutionary" insights that were revolutionary about twenty years ago.

But then Jürgen Dauk handed me this manuscript.

Here's what I expected to find: another collection of theoretical frameworks that look brilliant on whiteboards but crumble the moment you try to implement them in a real company with real people who have real problems. Another "proven system" that worked exactly once, in very specific circumstances, for a very specific company, but somehow promises to transform every organization on the planet.

Here's what I found: something different. Something that works.

You see, most business advice treats execution like it's a simple math problem. Step A plus Step B equals Success. If your company isn't performing, you must be doing the math wrong. Just follow the formula, they say. Implement the framework. Buy the software. Hire the consultants.

What these experts consistently miss – and what Jürgen gets right – is that execution isn't a math problem. It's a human problem. And humans, as anyone who's actually tried to run a business knows, are wonderfully, frustratingly unpredictable.

I've spent my career focused on one principle: stop trying to fix people's weaknesses and start amplifying their strengths. Most organizations waste enormous energy trying to turn introverts into extroverts, analytical minds into creative visionaries, or detail-oriented operators into big-picture strategists. It's like trying to teach a fish to climb a tree and then wondering why your aquarium isn't producing champion tree-climbers.

Jurgen understands this. More importantly, he's built an entire system around it.

What you'll find in these pages isn't just another business framework. It's a field guide for the messy, complex, infuriatingly human reality of getting things done in a world that changes faster than most companies can adapt.

The harsh realities Jürgen describes in Chapter 1? I've lived them. The execution gaps he identifies in Chapter 10? I've fallen into those chasms myself. The technology decisions that either amplify your competitive advantages or constrain them? I've made both kinds, sometimes in the same quarter.

But here's what makes this book different from the stack of business books collecting dust on your shelf: Jurgen has actually done this stuff. Not once, not in perfect conditions, but repeatedly, in the trenches, with real companies facing real constraints and real market pressures.

He's made the mistakes so you don't have to. He's tested the frameworks so you know they work. He's distilled the lessons so you can skip the expensive learning curve.

Take his insight about the difference between project thinking and product thinking. Most executives I know are still organizing their companies like it's 1995, building elaborate project plans that become obsolete before the ink dries. Meanwhile, their nimble competitors are thinking in products, iterating quickly, and adapting faster than traditional companies can hold planning meetings.

Or consider his approach to evidence-based decision making. In a world obsessed with "data-driven" everything, Jurgen makes a crucial distinction: being data-driven isn't enough if you're measuring the wrong things. Most companies have more dashboards than a Formula 1 race car and about as much clarity on whether they're actually winning.

The frameworks in this book aren't theoretical. They're practical. They're not elegant solutions for perfect companies; they're robust systems for the imperfect, chaotic, beautifully human organizations where most of us actually work.

Will this book solve all your problems? Of course not. Anyone who promises that is selling something, and you shouldn't buy it.

Will it give you a systematic approach to building and scaling technology companies that can execute their strategies? Absolutely.

Will it help you stop wasting time on initiatives that look impressive in PowerPoint but deliver nothing in practice? Without question.

Will it show you how to build organizations where people can do their best work instead of fighting the system just to get basic things done? That's exactly what it does.

I've watched too many brilliant leaders burn out trying to force square pegs into round holes, building companies that succeed despite their organizational design rather than because of it. Jurgen offers a better way.

The execution advantage isn't about working harder or moving faster. It's about building systems that amplify human potential instead of constraining it. It's about creating organizations that are designed for the reality of how work actually gets done, not the fantasy of how we wish it worked.

Most business books tell you what to think. This one shows you how to think systematically about the problems every scaling technology company faces.

The choice is yours. You can keep doing what you've always done and hope for different results. Or you can learn from someone who's figured out how to bridge the gap between strategic intention and operational reality.

I recommend the latter. Your future self will thank you.

P.S. - If you're one of those people who skips to the end to see if a book is worth reading, here's your answer: yes, it is. Now go back and actually read it. The frameworks don't implement themselves.

Introduction

You are a senior leader of a tech company. The market keeps changing. Competition is everywhere. And you're constantly asking: How do I grow this business without losing my soul?

I've spent twenty-five years in tech. I've seen companies succeed and fail. Most fail not because they lack talent or money. They fail because they forget why they exist.

This book isn't another business guide. It's a playbook for building companies that matter. Companies where people want to work. Companies that solve real problems. Companies that make money and meaning.

You might wonder why you should read this. Fair question. Most business books sit on shelves. Only 60% get opened. Only 20% get finished. Even fewer get used.

But here's why this one's different.

The tech industry is changing fast. The old rules don't work anymore. Building great products isn't enough. Having money isn't enough. You need something deeper.

This book comes from a simple truth: the best tech companies aren't the ones with cool products or big budgets. They're led by people who know that real success happens when profit meets enthusiastic people with passion, vision and purpose.

I've worked with startups that rapidly scaled. I've watched big companies reinvent themselves. I've also seen promising ventures die. Not from lack of talent. Not from lack of money. But because they lost their way.

What you'll find here isn't theory. It's real experience. Lessons from the trenches. Strategies that work. A blueprint for building companies that don't just survive but actually matter.

In the next chapters, we'll tackle seven problems I see everywhere in the industry:

1. No clear vision that unites everyone
2. Weak understanding of target customers and personas
3. Bad go-to-market strategies
4. People in wrong roles

5. Messy organizational structure
6. Lost focus on main goals
7. Poor use of technology

We won't just talk about these problems. We'll fix them. Each chapter gives you tools you can use right away. Real examples from real companies. Frameworks that work.

This book is a workbook. Use it. At the end of each chapter, you'll find questions and exercises. Do them. The value isn't in reading. It's in doing.

I know running a tech company is hard. The pressure is real. The stakes are high. Everything changes constantly. But I also know the potential you have.

When you finish this book, you'll see leadership differently. You'll have strategies for growth. You'll know how to build great teams. Most importantly, you'll have a plan for creating a company that succeeds and matters.

Ready to go beyond the usual thinking? To question what drives business success? To lead with vision and create lasting value?

The journey is tough, but the rewards are huge. Welcome to *The Leadership Operating System - A Playbook for Aligning Teams, Accelerating Growth and Dominating Markets*. Let's build a future in which profit and vision work together.

Why I Wrote This Book

It was after one of these executive business reviews where numbers didn't work out as planned, and instead of openly discussing the root cause, the usual blame game started. Everybody was defending their activities, cutbacks were proposed, and tighter review processes were announced.

I was sitting in a room full of senior executives. Each one looked frustrated and tired. Our teams were burning out, and the constant emergency mode of the last few quarters had been frustrating. This wasn't the first time I have been in such a situation and I felt exhausted.

I thought: there must be a better way. A way where great people are working towards a common goal. Where success and revenues are a natural result of inspired teams delivering world-class customer experiences. I realized the traditional business playbook wasn't working anymore. The landscape had shifted. The old maps were wrong.

This book is my answer to that question.

I've been a VP of operations, General Manager, and advisor to CEOs and founders. Each role taught me something new. More importantly, it showed me patterns. The same problems kept appearing in different companies.

These weren't random issues. They were systematic problems that hurt companies regardless of size or industry. I saw brilliant startups with amazing technology struggle to find customers. I watched established companies with deep pockets fail to adapt. Time after time, companies failed not because they lacked resources or talent but because something fundamental was wrong.

The more I looked, the more I saw a gap in how we think about success in tech. We had plenty of books on leadership. Lots of guides on technology strategy. No shortage of advice on operations. But something was missing. A complete approach that connected everything, based on a deeper sense of vision and purpose.

This sent me on a quest. I studied not just struggling companies but those that were winning against all odds. I interviewed hundreds of executives, from startup founders to senior leaders at big international companies. I studied research, went to conferences, and talked with thought leaders across many fields.

What I found was clear: seven critical problems consistently stood between companies and their potential. These weren't surface issues. They were deep problems that needed a fundamental shift in thinking.

Take the challenge of having a unifying vision. Over and over, I saw companies with talented teams and innovative products struggle because they lacked a clear, inspiring vision that could unite their workforce. Or consider misaligned talent. How often do we see brilliant people stuck in roles that don't use their real strengths?

But finding these problems was only half the work. The real question was: how do we fix them? And more questions followed. How do we build organizations that are profitable and purposeful? How do we create places where innovation thrives, where employees care deeply, and where success means more than just dollars? What if revenue growth and profit only reflect how well your employees thrive?

These questions became my focus. I experimented with new approaches in my work. Testing ideas. Refining strategies. Measuring results. I struggled, made mistakes, and learned. I worked with forward-thinking leaders who were willing to challenge conventional wisdom and try new ways of working. I discussed experiences with executives from various backgrounds leading change in mid-size and large companies. Slowly, a new framework emerged. One that didn't just address individual problems but provided a complete approach to building thriving, efficient, purpose-driven organizations.

This book is the result. It's everything I've learned, strategies I've tested, and insights I've gained from years of wrestling with the most pressing challenges in our industry. And it's more than best practices or theoretical concepts. It's a call to action. A challenge to rethink what leadership means in today's business world.

My goal isn't just to share knowledge but to inspire change. I want to give you the tools, frameworks, and mindsets you need to navigate our rapidly evolving industry. And more than that, I want to challenge you to think bigger. To look beyond short-term gains and consider the lasting impact you can have on your employees, your customers, and the world.

This book is for the visionary leader who senses there's more to business success than merely maximizing shareholder value. It's for the startup founder who wants to build a company that matters, not only one that makes money. It's for the seasoned executive who knows the old ways aren't working anymore and is ready to embrace a new approach.

We'll challenge assumptions, explore new ideas, and reimagine what it means to lead a successful technology company today. We'll explore practical strategies for addressing each of the seven critical challenges, backed by real examples and actionable advice.

This book isn't just about providing answers. It's about asking the right questions. It's about starting a conversation in our industry about what truly matters. About how we can use the incredible power of people and technology to create not just growth but meaning and value for employees, customers, and shareholders.

We're at the start of a new era in the technology industry. The choices we make as leaders will shape not only our companies but our digital society. My hope is that this book will guide and inspire those ready to lead toward a more sustainable, purposeful, and impactful future.

So, are you ready to go beyond just chasing profits? To explore a new way of leadership that balances profit with purpose and vision? To build a company that doesn't just chase short-term numbers but becomes a place where people are inspired and give their best every day to create value and delight customers? If so, let's turn the page and begin this journey.

Why That Matters to You

As a senior leader in tech, you might be wondering: "Why should this matter to me? How is this book different from all the other business advice out there?" These are valid questions. They get to the heart of why I believe this book isn't just relevant but crucial for your success in today's rapidly changing business world.

First, let's acknowledge your unique position. As a senior leader in a company, you're not just running a business. You're steering an organization at the forefront of technological innovation. Your decisions don't only impact your bottom line. They shape the digital infrastructure that powers our modern world. And they impact the lives of many people, inside and outside your organization. With this power comes responsibility and opportunity.

The challenges we face in our industry are unprecedented. The pace of technological change is mind-blowing. Artificial intelligence, blockchain, quantum computing - these aren't just buzzwords. They're paradigm-shifting technologies that redefine what's possible. On top of that, competition from growing tech nations and younger startups is emerging faster than ever. At the same time, we face complex ethical questions about data privacy, algorithmic bias, and the societal impact of our innovations. Hybrid work and changing talent expectations are only adding to the challenge.

In this context, the old playbook for business success is rapidly becoming obsolete. The strategies that brought you to where you are today may not be enough to take you where you need to go tomorrow. This is where "The Leadership Operating System" comes in. It's not just another set of tips for incremental improvement. It's fundamental rethinking of what it means to lead a successful tech company in the twenty-first century.

Let's look at the seven critical challenges we'll address. These aren't random topics. They're the result of years of observation and analysis of the most pressing issues facing our industry. Take the challenge of developing a unifying vision. In an era where top talent has more options than ever, having a clear, compelling vision and purpose isn't just nice to have. It's essential for attracting and retaining the best minds in the field and motivating them to give their best in their role.

Or take the challenge of misaligned talent. In our industry, human capital is everything. The difference between a good employee and a great one isn't just about productivity. It can be the difference between a product that succeeds and one that fails. Yet how many of us truly understand how to identify, nurture, and position our talent for maximum impact? And how many of us are reviewing how to best organize our people for maximum impact?

These challenges matter because they're directly tied to your ability to innovate, compete, and grow in an increasingly complex market. And more than that, they matter because they're at the heart of building a company that doesn't merely survive but thrives in the long term.

So why focus on meaning and purpose? Isn't profitability the ultimate goal of any business? Of course, financial success is crucial. Without it, we can't sustain our operations, invest in innovation, or reward our shareholders. But I'd argue that growth and profit are a natural outcome of a thriving organization, not a leading indicator of how well the business is doing.

Statistics show: 63% of millennials - who now make up the largest segment of the workforce - say the primary purpose of businesses should be "improving society" instead of "generating profit." Another survey found that 87% of customers would purchase a product or service because a company was truly great to work with and employees of that company were highly engaged. These aren't just feel-good statistics. They represent a fundamental shift in how people relate to businesses.

In our industry, where the war for talent is fierce, and where consumer trust is increasingly tied to customer experience, having a clear sense of purpose isn't just a bonus. It's a competitive advantage. It's what allows you to attract the brightest minds, inspire your team to do their best work, and build lasting relationships with your customers.

And here's the crucial point: purpose and profit aren't mutually exclusive. In fact, when properly aligned, they can create a powerful synergy that drives sustainable growth. We'll explore how companies that have successfully integrated purpose into their core strategy have not only achieved remarkable financial success but have also positioned themselves as leaders in their respective fields.

Take Salesforce, a company that has built its entire business model around stakeholder capitalism. By focusing not only on shareholder value, but on creating value for all stakeholders - employees, customers, partners, and communities - Salesforce has achieved phenomenal growth while also becoming known as one of the most innovative and socially responsible companies in the tech industry.

Or consider Microsoft's transformation under Satya Nadella's leadership. By refocusing the company around a mission to "empower every person and every organization on the planet to achieve more,"

Microsoft has not only revitalized its culture and product lineup but has also seen its market value soar.

These aren't isolated examples. A growing body of research shows that purpose-driven companies outperform their peers across a range of metrics, from employee engagement and customer loyalty to long-term financial performance.

This is why the ideas in this book matter. Because in today's world, leading with vision and purpose isn't just about doing good. It's about doing good business. It's about creating a sustainable competitive advantage in a rapidly changing market. It's about building a company that doesn't just weather the storms of disruption but thrives in the face of change.

We'll explore practical strategies for integrating vision and purpose into every aspect of your business - from strategic planning and product development to talent management and customer engagement. We'll look at how to overcome the common pitfalls that prevent companies from realizing their full potential, and we'll examine case studies of organizations that have successfully navigated these challenges.

Perhaps most importantly, we'll challenge you to think differently about your role as a leader. In a world where technology is reshaping every aspect of our lives, we have a unique opportunity and responsibility to shape that change for the better. By leading with vision and purpose, we can create companies that don't just generate profits but generate progress. Companies that don't just disrupt markets but improve lives.

This is the promise of "The Leadership Operating System" - a new way of leadership that balances profit with purpose, innovation with responsibility, and short-term gains with long-term impact. It's a challenging journey, but one that I believe is essential for any leader who wants to thrive in the technology industry of tomorrow.

So, as we look deeper into strategies and insights, I invite you to approach them not just as business techniques but as a roadmap for transformation - for your company and for yourself as a leader. Because implementing a new operating system isn't just about changing how we do business. It's about changing why we do business. And that's the key to unlocking unprecedented levels of success, fulfillment, and impact in our industry.

How to Best Use This Material

As we start this transformation journey, it's crucial to approach the material with the right mindset and strategy. "The Leadership Operating System" isn't just theories to passively consume. It's a practical guide designed to catalyze real change in your organization. To get the most out of this book, I recommend this approach:

1. Embrace an Open Mind

Some ideas may challenge your existing beliefs about leadership and business success. They may push you out of your comfort zone or contradict conventional wisdom. This is intentional. Real transformation often begins at the edge of our comfort zones, where we're willing to question our assumptions and explore new possibilities.

The technology industry is built on innovation - on looking at old problems in new ways. Apply this same innovative spirit to your approach to leadership and organizational development. Be willing to experiment, to try new ideas, and to learn from both successes and failures.

2. Reflect and Apply

You'll find reflection questions and practical exercises at the end of each chapter. These aren't just academic exercises. They're designed to help you apply the concepts directly to your unique situation. Take the time to engage with these deeply. Set aside dedicated time to work through them, ideally in a quiet space where you can think without interruptions.

Consider keeping a journal as you work through the book. Use it to record your thoughts, observations, ideas, and insights. This will not only help you internalize the material but will also serve as a valuable resource as you implement changes in your organization.

3. Involve Your Team

While you can certainly work through this material on your own, the real power comes when you involve your leadership team. Consider using the chapters as a framework for strategic planning sessions or leadership retreats. Encourage your team to read along and discuss the ideas in regular meetings.

By involving your team, you're not just gaining diverse perspectives on the material. You're also building buy-in for the changes you'll implement. Transformational change isn't something that can be dictated from the top down. It requires engagement and commitment at all levels.

4. Start Small, but Start Now

You'll likely find yourself buzzing with ideas for change. While this enthusiasm is great, it's important not to try to change everything at once. Instead, focus on implementing one or two key ideas from each chapter. Start with small, manageable changes that can create quick wins and build momentum.

For example, after reading about the importance of a unifying vision, you might start by holding workshops with your leadership team to refine and articulate your company's purpose. Or after exploring the challenge of misaligned talent, you could begin by reassessing the roles and responsibilities of key team members.

The key is to start now. Don't wait until you've finished the entire book to implement changes. Each small step you take is a step toward transforming your organization.

5. Measure and Iterate

As you implement changes, it's crucial to measure their impact. Set clear metrics for success and regularly assess your progress. This could involve quantitative measures like employee engagement scores or customer satisfaction ratings, as well as qualitative feedback from your team and stakeholders.

Be prepared to iterate on your approach. Not every strategy will work perfectly the first time, and that's okay. The goal is continuous improvement, not instant perfection. Use the feedback you gather to refine your approach and adjust as needed.

6. Create a Learning Culture

As you work through this material, strive to create a culture of continuous learning in your organization. Encourage your team to share insights, discuss challenges, and propose new ideas. Consider setting up a regular forum where team members can share what they learn and how they apply new concepts.

The goal isn't to implement a set of strategies but to cultivate a mindset of purpose-driven leadership throughout your organization. By fostering a learning culture, you set the stage for ongoing growth and adaptation.

7. Personalize the Approach

While the strategies have been proven effective across a range of organizations, it's important to adapt them to your specific context. Your company's size, culture, market position, and unique challenges will influence how you apply these concepts.

Don't be afraid to experiment and find what works best for your organization. The goal is not to follow a rigid formula but to use these ideas as a springboard for developing your unique approach to purpose-driven leadership.

8. Be Patient and Persistent

Transformational change doesn't happen overnight. It's a journey that requires patience, persistence, and a long-term perspective. There will be setbacks and challenges along the way. You may face resistance from team members who are comfortable with the status quo. You may encounter unexpected obstacles as you try to implement new strategies.

Don't let these challenges discourage you. Remember why you started this journey in the first place - to create a more purposeful, impactful, and successful organization. Keep your eye on the long-term vision, even as you navigate short-term difficulties.

9. Share Your Journey

As you implement these ideas and start seeing results, consider sharing your experiences with others in the industry. Whether through speaking engagements, blog posts, or informal conversations with peers, sharing your journey can help inspire others and contribute to a broader shift toward purpose-driven leadership in the technology industry.

10. Revisit and Refresh

Finally, remember that this book is not a one-time read but a resource to return to again and again. As your organization evolves and faces new challenges, different aspects of the material may become more relevant. Plan to revisit the book regularly, perhaps on an annual basis, to refresh your understanding and find new insights.

By approaching this material with intention, openness, and a commitment to action, you're not just reading a book. You're embarking on a transformative journey. A journey that has the potential to not only elevate your organization but also to redefine what success looks like in our industry.

The Seven Critical Challenges

As we go deeper into "The Leadership Operating System," it's crucial to understand the landscape we're navigating. Through years of observation, research, and hands-on experience, I've identified seven critical challenges that consistently hinder the growth and success of technology companies. These aren't just surface-level issues but deep-rooted obstacles that require a paradigm shift to overcome. Let's explore each of these challenges briefly, setting the stage for the in-depth strategies we'll discuss in the coming chapters.

1. Missing "North Star" Vision

In the fast-paced world of technology, it's easy to get caught up in day-to-day operations, losing sight of the bigger picture. Many companies lack a clear, compelling vision that goes beyond profit - a "North Star" that guides every decision and inspires every team member. Without this unifying purpose, organizations often find themselves adrift, struggling to maintain focus and motivation in the face of challenges.

Consider a mid-sized software company I worked with. Despite having talented engineers and innovative products, they struggled with high turnover and flat market performance. When we looked into the details, we discovered that employees didn't feel they were contributing to something meaningful. They couldn't articulate why their work mattered beyond meeting quarterly targets. To the surprise of the CEO, twenty out of twenty interviewed employees could not tell what the vision or mission of the company was. By developing a clear, purpose-driven vision, the company not only improved employee engagement but also found new avenues for growth aligned with their core values.

2. Weak Ideal Customer Profile and Persona Development

In an industry where creating customer value and user experience are paramount, many companies still have a very limited understanding of their ideal customer profile and the different personas within their ICP. They fail to clearly define and understand their target customers in detail or develop detailed buyer personas, resulting in unfocused marketing efforts and products that don't fully meet customer needs and therefore don't provide the biggest possible customer value.

I recently consulted for a startup that had developed a powerful data analytics tool. Despite its capabilities, the product wasn't gaining traction. We found they were trying to be everything to everyone, diluting their message and confusing potential customers. By honing in on specific industries and developing detailed personas, they were able to tailor their product offering and marketing messaging, leading to a significant uptick in adoption.

3. Wrong Go-to-Market Strategies

Even the most innovative product can fail if it's not brought to market effectively. Many technology companies struggle with crafting and executing a cohesive go-to-market strategy. This often results in high customer acquisition cost, low conversion rates, low profitability, and a failure to gain market share.

A classic example is a software vendor I worked with. They had a great solution that was solving a specific pain for CFOs of mid-sized companies. Upon investigation, we found their go-to-market strategy was inefficient. They were using a costly enterprise direct sales motion while their average deal size within their mid-sized company target market was quite low. By shifting to a white label distribution model, they were able to rapidly increase their new logo signings while reducing their customer acquisition cost.

4. Inefficient Organizational Structure

Market conditions change at an increasing speed and the ability to be business agile is key to survive and thrive. Traditional matrix-style organizations that were built for command and control are becoming a burden in today's fast-paced world, as they are inefficient and slow to adapt to changing requirements and market conditions. In reality, matrix-structured companies are usually siloed organizations with misaligned priorities and goals. This leads to inefficiencies, duplicated efforts, and gaps in critical processes. Moreover, it often creates frustration among team members and hinders accountability.

I recall a rapidly growing SaaS firm that was struggling with project delays and quality issues and churning customers. When we interviewed team members of different functions such as sales, consulting, support, and customer success, we quickly found out that each function was working toward different goals and not acting as one cohesive team. In an experiment, a small team with members of each function was put in place and given a joint team goal. The results were eye-opening. Within two weeks, the small new team figured out how to best bring their set of customers back on track and how to organize themselves in the most efficient way to achieve this.

5. Misalignment of Talent and Positions

One of the most common issues I've encountered is the misplacement of key personnel. This often manifests as putting strategic thinkers in tactical roles or vice versa. Such misalignment not only leads to underperformance but can also result in the loss of top talent.

I worked with a CTO who was brilliant at developing innovative solutions but struggled with the day-to-day management of his team. By shifting his focus to a chief innovation officer role and bringing in a more operationally-focused CTO, the company was able to leverage his strengths while improving overall department performance.

6. Lack of Focus on Primary Goals

In many organizations, the focus is scattered across numerous initiatives, often resulting in a loss of sight of the primary goal. I've seen salespeople spending only 10 to 15% of their time selling, and managers dedicating a mere 10% to coaching their teams. This diffusion of effort can severely impact a company's ability to achieve its core objectives.

An enterprise software company I advised was launching new features at a breakneck pace, believing this was the key to staying competitive. However, this frenetic activity was leading to buggy releases and customer dissatisfaction. By refocusing on their primary goal of solving specific customer pain points, they were able to slow down, improve quality, and ultimately increase customer satisfaction and retention.

7. Inadequate Leveraging of Technology

In an ironic twist, many software and IT companies fail to fully leverage technology within their own operations. Too often, technology is used primarily for tracking and controlling employees, rather than enhancing productivity and customer satisfaction. Best-in-class companies implement IT expertise within their business teams so they can work together on how to best leverage technology to best serve the business and their customers.

I encountered this with a tech scale-up firm that had a growing IT department that was separate from other business functions. IT was seen as a cost center rather than a business enabler. By implementing IT within the business rather than outside, the newly formed teams quickly implemented solutions that increased productivity by over 15% within the first year.

These seven challenges form the core of what we'll address. They are interconnected, often reinforcing each other in ways that can create a vicious cycle of underperformance. However, by tackling them head-on with a purpose-driven approach, we can transform them into opportunities for growth and innovation.

Charting Your Course Beyond Greed

As we conclude this introduction to The Leadership Operating System - A Playbook for Aligning Teams, Accelerating Growth, and Dominating Markets, let's take a moment to reflect on the journey ahead.

The path we're about to embark on might not be easy. It requires courage to challenge the status quo, wisdom to see beyond short-term gains, and resilience to persevere in the face of obstacles. But the rewards - for you, your team, your customers, and society at large - are immeasurable.

We'll look into each of the seven challenges, providing you with practical strategies, real-world examples, and actionable insights. You'll learn how to craft a compelling vision that galvanizes your entire organization. We'll explore techniques for precise market targeting and persona development that will sharpen your competitive edge. You'll discover how to create and execute flawless go-to-market strategies that drive growth and innovation.

We'll tackle the sensitive issues of role clarity and talent alignment, showing you how to build a high-performing team where every individual is positioned to excel. You'll learn how to maintain laser-like focus on your primary goals, even amidst the chaos and complexity of the tech industry. And we'll explore how to leverage technology not just as a product you sell, but as a force multiplier within your own organization.

But more than simply addressing these individual challenges, this book aims to fundamentally shift your perspective on what it means to lead a successful tech company in the twenty-first century. It's about recognizing that in today's world, purpose and profit are not opposing forces but complementary drivers of sustainable success.

I encourage you to approach this material with an open mind and a willingness to challenge your assumptions. These strategies and insights aren't merely theoretical concepts. They're battle-tested approaches that have helped companies like yours overcome significant obstacles and achieve remarkable success.

The goal isn't perfection but progress. Each step you take toward more purposeful leadership is a step toward building a more resilient, innovative, and impactful organization. It's about creating a company that doesn't just weather the storms of disruption but thrives in the face of change.

Here are five action steps to get you started on your journey beyond greed:

Reflect on Your Current State:

Take an honest assessment of where your company stands in relation to the seven challenges we've discussed. Where do you see the greatest opportunities for improvement?

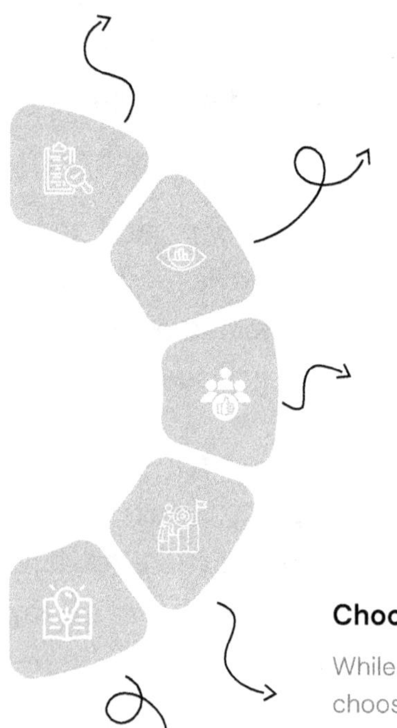

Articulate Your Why:

Begin the process of defining or refining your company's vision. Why does your organization exist beyond making money? Why would employees work for your company beyond salary?

Engage Your Team:

Share the concepts from this introduction with your leadership team. Gauge their reactions and invite their perspectives on how these ideas might apply to your organization.

Choose One Challenge to Tackle:

While we'll be addressing all seven challenges in depth, choose one that resonates most strongly with your current situation. Commit to focusing on this area as you work through the book.

Set Aside Learning Time:

Block out regular time in your schedule to engage with this material. Whether it's an hour each week or a monthly deep-dive session, commit to making this journey a priority.

TEMPLATES

I want to leave you with a thought: the future of the technology industry - indeed, the future of business itself - will be shaped by leaders who understand that true success lies in the harmony of purpose and profit. By embarking on this journey, you're not just transforming your own organization. You're helping to create a new paradigm of leadership for our digital age.

The challenges ahead are significant, but so are the opportunities. With the right mindset, strategies, and commitment, you have the power to build a company that doesn't just succeed financially, but makes a lasting, positive impact on employees and customers.

Are you ready to start the transformation journey? To lead with purpose, innovate with meaning, and create value that transcends the bottom line? If so, then let's turn the page and begin this transformative journey together. The future of purposeful leadership in tech starts here, with you, right now.

01

CHAPTER

The Harsh Reality of Today's Businesses

I was sitting in a conference room in London Stratford. I flew in early morning, had a couple of coffees and knew this would be another tough day. The CEO across from me looked exhausted. His company used to be a star investment. Now it was struggling.

"I don't get it," he said quietly. "We're doing everything right. Great people, good technology, strong market position. But we're way behind our plan. Customers are unhappy. Employees don't care. Investors are getting nervous. How did this happen?"

This happens everywhere. In boardrooms around the world, from new startups to big established companies. The hard truth? Success isn't guaranteed anymore. Not even for the best players. The game keeps changing. What worked yesterday might kill you tomorrow.

John D. Rockefeller said it best: "If you want to succeed, you should strike out on new paths, rather than travel the worn paths of accepted success." This is truer today than ever, especially in tech where disruption isn't just a buzzword. It's daily reality.

Here's a shocking fact: 95% of tech industry profits go to just 20% of companies. This isn't just about big companies winning. It's about the growing gap between those who adapt and those who stick to old ways. With the rapid evolution of AI this gap will only widen.

So, what are these harsh realities that even successful businesses struggle with? Let's break them down:

01

Digital Disruption:

Every industry is getting disrupted by digital technology. Finance, healthcare, retail - you name it. Companies that don't embrace digital and organizational transformation get beaten by more agile competitors.

02

Fast-Changing Markets:

Stable, predictable markets are gone. Today, you're navigating constant change. Customer preferences shift. Technology advances. Global events can flip the playing field overnight.

03

The Acquisition Problem:

With high interest rates, growing through acquisitions is getting expensive. Companies need new ways to expand, or they'll stagnate.

04 **The Agility Gap:**

Business agility isn't nice to have anymore. It's survival. But many established companies are stuck with old systems and slow processes.

05 **The Productivity Problem:**

Despite all our technology, many businesses are seeing productivity drop. Information overload and misaligned incentives are big challenges.

06 **The Strategy-Execution Divide:**

Great strategies mean nothing if you can't execute them. Many companies have a "strategic black hole" – the gap between boardroom plans and what actually happens.

These challenges connect. They feed off each other. They create a complex web that demands a complete approach, not quick fixes.

Think about your own company. How many of these challenges sound familiar? Are you seeing unhappy customers? Disengaged employees? Missed growth targets? These aren't just symptoms of a struggling business. They're wake-up calls telling you to rethink how you lead, innovate, and create value.

Throughout this chapter, we'll analyze these challenges with real examples and data. More importantly, we'll map out how to overcome them. We'll lay the groundwork for building a more resilient, agile, and purpose-driven organization.

Acknowledging these harsh realities isn't giving up. It's the first step toward real change. As we go through this, I challenge you to approach these insights with an open mind. Be willing to question long-held beliefs about what drives business success.

The Customer Mystery

In the rush to grow and make money, many businesses have lost sight of their most valuable asset: their customers. The harsh reality? Customers are increasingly unhappy, frustrated, and skeptical of companies they once supported. This isn't a small setback. It's a ticking time bomb that threatens the foundation of business sustainability.

Back to our London CEO. He pulls up a chart on his tablet. "Look at these numbers," he says, disbelief in his voice. "Customer satisfaction scores dropped 30% in just one year. We're losing clients faster than we can find new ones. What's happening?"

This scene plays out across industries all the time. The root problem? A fundamental disconnect between what businesses think customers want and what customers actually need. In our drive to optimize processes, cut costs, and boost short-term profits, we've lost touch with the human side of business - the relationships, experiences, and emotions that drive customer loyalty. Our daily operation is centered more around our own internal needs than around serving our customers in the best possible way.

Take Captarion, a software company that used to thrive. To save money, they outsourced customer support to a provider halfway around the world. On paper, it looked brilliant - millions in cost savings annually.

Reality was different. Within months, customer complaints exploded. Response times lagged. Cultural misunderstandings became normal. The technical support customers expected was replaced by scripted responses and endless queues. The result? Long-time clients left in droves. Their reputation went from industry leader to cautionary tale almost overnight.

This shows a critical point: customers aren't just seeking products or services. They want value, understanding, and partnership. When businesses put cost-cutting over customer experience, they're trading long-term sustainability for short-term gains.

And the customer problem goes deeper than just poor service. It's about how businesses see and interact with their customers. Too often, customers feel like walking wallets rather than valued partners. This transactional mindset creates a gap between businesses and customers, eroding trust and loyalty over time. In today's world, business customers expect the same level of service and the same customer experience that they are used to as private consumer.

Listen to Sarah, a long-time client of a major software provider I worked for: "I've been with them for over ten years, but lately, it feels like they don't even know who I am. Every interaction is an upsell opportunity. They don't seem interested in understanding my business challenges or how their product fits our strategy. It's all about the next upgrade, the next add-on. Their quarter end is more important than my project deadlines. I feel like a number, not a partner."

Sarah's frustration echoes what customers across industries are feeling. They're tired of being treated as data points in a CRM system. They want real relationships, personalized experiences, and a sense that the companies they support care about their success.

This disconnect gets worse with rapid technological change. As businesses rush to adopt AI, machine learning, and automation, they often do so at the expense of human touch. While these innovations can enhance customer experiences, they also create barriers if not implemented thoughtfully.

For example, over-relying on chatbots and automated support can leave customers feeling frustrated and unheard, especially with complex issues that need nuanced understanding. The key is finding the right balance between technological efficiency and human empathy - a balance many businesses struggle to find.

And in the age of social media and instant communication, customer dissatisfaction spreads like wildfire. One negative experience, amplified through digital channels, can damage a brand's reputation in ways that would have been impossible decades ago. This reality demands customer-centricity that goes beyond lip service and touches every part of business operations.

So, how do we start addressing this customer conundrum? The first step is recognition - admitting there's a problem that needs more than surface fixes. It demands a fundamental shift in how we view and value our customers.

This shift starts with empathy - truly putting ourselves in our customers' shoes. It means going beyond demographic data and purchase histories to understand the real-world challenges, aspirations, and contexts that drive customer behavior. It requires asking tough questions: Are we creating genuine value for our customers or just pushing products? Are we listening to their feedback and evolving accordingly, or are we stuck in our own echo chamber?

I'm always surprised how rarely companies check in with their customers to understand the value they're getting from their solution. Do you know whether your customers are actually seeing the ROI that was promised? Did they achieve what they calculated internally? Most software companies don't even track what was promised.

We'll explore practical strategies for reconnecting with customers in meaningful ways. We'll look at how leading companies use technology not to replace human interaction, but to enhance it. We'll examine the power of personalization, the importance of transparency, and the critical role of continuous feedback loops in building lasting customer relationships.

In today's hyper-competitive landscape, customer satisfaction isn't just nice to have - it's a fundamental driver of business success. As we navigate the complexities of the digital age, those who can authentically connect with their customers, understand their evolving needs, and consistently deliver value will be the ones who don't just survive but thrive.

Customer dissatisfaction is real, but it's not permanent. By recognizing the problem and committing to a customer-centric approach, we can bridge the gap between business objectives and customer needs, paving the way for sustainable growth and long-term success.

As Sundar Pichai, CEO of Google said: "Follow the user, and all else will follow."

The Employee Engagement Crisis

As we turn our focus inward, we face another harsh reality plaguing today's businesses: the crisis of employee disengagement. This issue, while less visible than customer dissatisfaction, is equally damaging to an organization's health and long-term viability. It's a silent epidemic that's draining productivity, stifling innovation, and undermining the foundations of corporate success.

Back to our worried London CEO. As he struggles with plummeting customer satisfaction scores, another blow hits: the annual employee engagement survey results. The numbers are terrible - only 20% of employees report feeling engaged in their work, a sharp drop from previous years. Even worse, many top performers are actively looking for jobs elsewhere.

This scenario isn't unique. Recent studies show that only about one-third of U.S. employees report being engaged at work. The rest are either not engaged or, worse, actively disengaged. The cost of this disengagement is staggering - estimated at up to $550 billion annually in lost productivity for U.S. companies alone.

So, what's driving this engagement crisis? The answer lies in a complex web of factors, many stemming from fundamental misalignments between organizational practices and employee needs and expectations.

Consider Quotruent, a mid-sized software company that prided itself on its "innovative" culture. On the surface, Quotruent seemed to have it all – ping-pong tables in the break room, free snacks, and regular team-building events. The company's social media showcased photos of smiling employees and hashtags about work-life balance.

Yet beneath this surface of workplace satisfaction, a different story was unfolding. Employees were burning out at an alarming rate. Many reported feeling overwhelmed, underappreciated, and disconnected from the company's mission. Despite the trappings of a "fun" work environment, people were leaving in droves, taking valuable knowledge and skills with them.

What went wrong? Quotruent, like many companies, had fallen into the trap of confusing perks with purpose. They had invested in superficial elements of workplace culture without addressing the deeper needs of their employees - needs for meaningful work, professional growth, and a sense of belonging to something greater than themselves.

The people and culture team was more focused on creating great social media content than talking to employees on the ground. Otherwise, they would have spotted that people are stressed out by conflicting priorities and orders, are spending 80% of their work time on internal video calls, and don't feel their challenges are recognized and addressed. Seeing happy social media posts only comes as a joke.

This misalignment between what companies offer and what employees truly need is at the heart of the engagement crisis. Today's workforce, particularly millennials and Gen Z, are seeking more than just a paycheck. They want purpose, impact, and the opportunity to grow both personally and professionally. They want to understand how they can contribute to achieving a vision, and they want a workplace that supports them in doing so.

Moreover, the nature of work itself is changing rapidly, adding another layer of complexity to the engagement puzzle. The rise of remote work, accelerated by the global pandemic, has blurred the lines between work and personal life. While offering flexibility, it has also created new challenges in fostering connection and maintaining work-life balance. I have seen many companies where more time is spent on alignment calls than on actual work.

Take the experience of Mark, a software developer at a large tech firm: "I used to love my job. The work was challenging, and I felt like I was making a real difference. But lately, it's like I'm just a cog in a machine. I'm constantly in reactive mode, putting out fires instead of innovating. Most of my time is spent on internal bureaucracy rather than actual coding. I feel disconnected from my team and the company's mission. Some days, I wonder why I even bother logging in."

Mark's sentiment echoes that of countless employees across industries. They're stressed, overwhelmed, and increasingly questioning the role of work in their lives. This disengagement isn't merely a personal issue - it has profound implications for business performance and innovation.

Disengaged employees are less productive, less creative, and less likely to go the extra mile for customers. They're also more prone to errors and more likely to engage in counterproductive workplace behaviors. In an industry where human capital is everything, this erosion of engagement is nothing short of a crisis.

Furthermore, in the age of social media and company review sites like Glassdoor, employee dissatisfaction can quickly become public, damaging a company's employer brand and making it harder to attract top talent. It's a vicious cycle that can cripple even the most promising organizations.

So, how do we begin to address this engagement crisis? The first step, as with the customer conundrum, is recognition. We must acknowledge that employee engagement is not an HR issue, but a core business challenge that demands attention at the highest levels of leadership.

Next, we need to rethink what engagement truly means in today's context. It's not about perks or ping-pong tables. It's about creating an environment where employees feel valued, heard, and connected to a larger purpose. It's about aligning individual aspirations with organizational goals, and providing opportunities for growth and meaningful contribution.

This rethinking requires a fundamental shift in how we view the employer-employee relationship. Instead of seeing employees as resources to be optimized, we need to see them as partners in value creation. This means involving them in decision-making processes, providing transparency about company direction, and creating pathways for professional development and career progression.

It also means addressing the root causes of stress and burnout. Many companies have unwittingly created cultures of overwork and constant connectivity, where employees feel pressured to be "always on." Reversing this trend requires not just policy changes, but a shift in mindset at all levels of the organization and a re-evaluation of the organizational structure.

We'll explore practical strategies for rekindling employee engagement. We'll look at how leading companies create cultures of purpose and belonging. We'll examine the role of leadership in fostering engagement and the importance of aligning organizational systems and processes with employee needs.

In the knowledge economy, engaged employees are your most valuable asset. They're the source of innovation, the face of your brand to customers, and the key to sustainable competitive advantage. Addressing the engagement crisis isn't just about making people feel good - it's about unleashing the full potential of your workforce to drive business success.

The road to re-engagement may be challenging, but it's a journey that no forward-thinking organization can afford to ignore. By recognizing the problem and committing to meaningful change, we can bridge the gap between employee expectations and organizational realities, creating workplaces that are not just productive but truly fulfilling.

The Growth Gap - Missed Targets and Market Realities

As we dig deeper into the harsh realities facing today's businesses, we encounter a challenge that keeps many CEOs awake at night: the persistent gap between projected growth and actual performance. This "growth gap" isn't only about missed targets. It's a symptom of a deeper disconnect between strategic aspirations and market realities.

Let's revisit our London CEO one more time. He's staring at a graph that tells a sobering story. The company's actual growth rate is barely half of what was projected at the beginning of the year. The carefully planned new product ramp up doesn't materialize anywhere close to projected numbers. "We had such high hopes," he mutters, shaking his head. "Where did we go wrong?"

This scenario is distressingly common. In fact, research shows that CEOs routinely forecast double the growth they actually achieve and close to four times the profitability. These aren't just minor miscalculations. They represent a fundamental misalignment between expectations and reality that can have far-reaching consequences for businesses.

Consider the statistic we mentioned earlier: 95% of profits in the software and IT sector are earned by the top 20% of companies. This concentration of success isn't only about market dominance. It's a reflection of how challenging sustainable growth has become in today's rapidly evolving business landscape.

Take the warning example of Ration, once a dominant player in enterprise software. Riding high on past successes, Ration's leadership set ambitious growth targets year after year. They projected double-digit growth based on historical performance and market size. However, they failed to account for several critical factors:

1. Rapid technological shifts that made their core products increasingly obsolete
2. The emergence of cloud-based solutions that disrupted their traditional licensing model
3. Changing customer preferences towards more agile, user-friendly interfaces

As a result, Ration not only missed its growth targets but saw its market share steadily erode. By the time they recognized the severity of the problem, they were already playing catch-up in a market they once dominated.

This example shows a crucial point: in today's business environment, past performance is no longer a reliable predictor of future success. The pace of change is so rapid, and disruption so widespread, that even the most established companies can find themselves suddenly out of step with market realities.

Some of the biggest names in technology are warning examples. Think of brands like Kodak, once dominating the photo film industry, or Blackberry, the once-leading business mobile phone.

So, what's driving this persistent growth gap? Several factors come into play:

01 **Overoptimism Bias:**

There's a natural tendency among leaders to be overly optimistic about their company's prospects. This can lead to unrealistic projections and strategies that aren't grounded in market realities.

02 **Failure to Anticipate Disruption:**

Many companies underestimate the potential impact of new technologies or business models on their industry. They assume the rules that governed their past success will continue to apply.

03 **Misalignment Between Strategy and Execution:**

Even well-crafted strategies can fail if there's a disconnect between high-level plans and on-the-ground execution. This "strategy-execution gap" is a common issue in missed growth targets.

04 **Inadequate Market Intelligence:**

In a rapidly changing business environment, companies often lack real-time insights into market trends, customer preferences, and competitive dynamics. A common trap is also making assumptions on data and not verifying assumptions by talking to customers. This information lag can lead to misguided strategies and missed opportunities.

---

05 **Resistance to Change:**

Established companies often struggle with organizational inertia. They may recognize the need for change intellectually but focus on short term "quick fixes" rather than long term transformation.

The consequences of this growth gap extend far beyond missed financial targets. It can lead to loss of investor confidence, talent drain, and a downward spiral of declining competitiveness. Moreover, in an attempt to close this gap, companies may resort to short-term measures that further compromise their long-term viability.

For instance, faced with missed growth targets, companies might slash R&D budgets, cut back on employee training, or engage in aggressive cost-cutting measures. While these actions might provide a temporary boost to the bottom line, they often come at the expense of innovation, employee morale, and long-term competitiveness.

So, how can businesses bridge this growth gap? The first step is to cultivate a more realistic and nuanced approach to growth projections and strategy formulation. This involves:

01 **Embracing Data-Driven Decision Making:**
Using advanced analytics and market intelligence tools to gain real-time insights into market trends and customer behavior.

02 **Developing Scenario-Based Strategies:**
Instead of relying on single-point forecasts, companies should develop flexible strategies that can adapt to various potential future scenarios.

03 **Fostering a Culture of Agility:**
Building organizational structures and processes that can quickly pivot in response to market changes.

04 **Aligning Incentives with Long-Term Growth:**
Ensuring that compensation and performance metrics encourage sustainable growth rather than short-term gains.

05 **Investing in Innovation:**
Maintaining a strong focus on R&D and new product development, even in the face of short-term pressures.

Moreover, companies need to rethink how they measure and define success. In a world of rapid change and disruption, traditional metrics like year-over-year growth or market share may not tell the full story.

Instead, companies should consider metrics that reflect their ability to innovate, adapt, and create long-term value for customers and stakeholders.

As we continue our exploration of the harsh realities facing today's businesses, it's clear that the growth gap is not just a financial challenge - it's a strategic imperative that demands a fundamental rethinking of how we approach business growth and success.

In the next section, we'll look into another critical challenge that often widens the growth gap: the tension between short-term profits and long-term sustainability. This balancing act lies at the heart of many of the difficulties faced by established businesses in today's dynamic marketplace.

The Profit Paradox - Short-Term Gains vs. Long-Term Sustainability

As we navigate deeper into the harsh realities of today's business landscape, we encounter a tension that lies at the heart of many corporate struggles: the conflict between short-term profitability and long-term sustainability. This "profit paradox" is perhaps one of the most insidious challenges facing established businesses, often leading to decisions that boost immediate returns at the expense of future viability.

Let's return one last time to our London CEO. He faces intense pressure from investors to improve quarterly results. The board is pushing for cost-cutting measures and a focus on high-margin products. Yet, he knows these actions could compromise the company's ability to innovate and compete in the long run. "How do I balance what the market wants today with what the company needs for tomorrow?" he wonders aloud.

This dilemma is far from unique. In fact, it's a systemic issue in today's corporate world, driven by a combination of market pressures, misaligned incentives, and short-term thinking. The consequences of this short-termism are profound and far-reaching, affecting everything from innovation and employee morale to customer satisfaction and long-term competitiveness.

Reflect on the case of Erpion, a once-leading software company. Under pressure to meet quarterly earnings targets, Erpion's leadership made a series of decisions aimed at boosting short-term profits:

1. They slashed their R&D budget, focusing resources on marketing legacy solutions rather than driving development on their new platform.
2. They pushed discounted long-term renewals, maximizing revenue from their current portfolio.
3. They implemented aggressive cost-cutting measures, including significant layoffs in research and development departments.

In the short term, these moves paid off. Erpion's stock price soared, and they exceeded earnings expectations for several quarters. However, the long-term consequences were severe. Within a few quarters, their pipeline of new customers had dried up. They lost market share to more innovative competitors. Their reputation suffered as customers were locked in with technology that was falling behind. What seemed like smart business moves in the moment had set the stage for a long-term decline.

This example shows a crucial point: the decisions that boost profits today can often undermine the foundations of future success. It's a trap that many companies fall into, driven by a combination of external pressures and internal short-sightedness.

So, what's driving this profit paradox? Several factors come into play:

Shareholder/Investor Pressure:

The demand for consistent quarterly growth from shareholders and analysts can push companies towards short-term thinking.

Executive Compensation Structures:

When executive bonuses are tied primarily to short-term financial metrics, it creates incentives for decisions that boost immediate results at the expense of long-term value creation.

Competitive Pressures:

In fast-moving industries, there's often a fear that focusing on long-term initiatives will leave a company vulnerable to more agile competitors in the short term.

Misalignment of Metrics:

Many companies still rely heavily on traditional financial metrics that don't capture leading indicators on long-term value creation or sustainability.

Cognitive Biases:

Human tendency towards immediate gratification can influence corporate decision-making, leading to a preference for short-term gains over long-term benefits.

The consequences of this short-term focus extend far beyond financial statements. It can lead to a culture of risk aversion, where bold, innovative ideas are shelved in favor of incremental improvements that can deliver more predictable short-term results. It can demoralize employees, particularly those engaged in long-term projects or research. And perhaps most critically, it can erode a company's ability to adapt and evolve in response to changing market conditions.

Moreover, this short-term focus often creates a vicious cycle. As companies prioritize immediate results, they may underinvest in areas crucial for long-term success - things like employee development, customer relationship building, and foundational research. This underinvestment makes it harder to achieve growth in the future, increasing the pressure for short-term measures, and so the cycle continues.

So, how can businesses break free from this profit paradox and strike a balance between short-term performance and long-term sustainability? Several strategies can help:

1. **Redefine Success Metrics:**

   Implement a balanced scorecard approach that includes short-term financial metrics and long-term value creation indicators. This might include measures of innovation output, customer loyalty, employee engagement, and sustainability.

2. **Align Incentives:**

   Restructure executive compensation to include long-term performance metrics and tie a portion of bonuses to achieving strategic, non-financial goals.

3. **Communicate a Long-Term Vision:**

   Clearly articulate a compelling long-term vision to stakeholders, including shareholders. Companies like Amazon have successfully convinced investors to prioritize long-term growth over short-term profits.

4. **Invest in Strategic Foresight:**

   Develop robust scenario planning and foresight capabilities to anticipate future market changes and align current decisions with long-term trends.

5. **Foster a Culture of Innovation:**

   Create safe spaces for experimentation and calculated risk-taking within the organization. This can help balance the need for predictable short-term results with the pursuit of breakthrough innovations.

6. **Embrace Stakeholder Capitalism:**

   Expand the definition of corporate success to include value creation for all stakeholders - employees, customers, communities, and the environment - not just shareholders.

7. **Practice Transparent Reporting:**

   Provide clear, comprehensive reporting on short-term performance and long-term value creation initiatives. This can help educate investors and analysts about the importance of balancing short and long-term goals.

It's important to note that balancing short-term performance with long-term sustainability isn't about ignoring short-term results. Rather, it's about making decisions that create value in the short term while also laying the groundwork for future success.

Companies that successfully navigate this balance often exhibit a few key traits:

1. They have a clear, compelling long-term vision that guides decision-making at all levels of the organization.
2. They maintain a consistent investment in core capabilities and innovation, even during downturns.
3. They actively manage investor expectations, educating the market about their long-term strategy and the metrics that matter.
4. They cultivate a diverse ecosystem of stakeholders, recognizing that long-term success depends on creating value for customers, employees, and communities, not just shareholders.

As we wrap up our exploration of the harsh realities facing today's businesses, it's clear the profit paradox presents a significant challenge and an opportunity. Those who can successfully balance short-term performance with long-term value creation will be best positioned to thrive in an increasingly complex and rapidly changing business environment.

In our final section, we'll synthesize the insights from all these challenges and outline a path forward for leaders looking to build truly resilient, sustainable, and successful organizations in the face of these harsh realities.

Confronting Harsh Realities

It's clear the challenges are multifaceted and interconnected. From the customer mystery and employee engagement crisis to the growth gap and the profit paradox, these issues form a complex web that can entangle even the most seasoned business leaders. However, within these challenges lie opportunities for transformation and sustainable success.

Let's take a moment to synthesize what we've learned and chart a course forward. The challenges we've covered are uncomfortable, but they offer great potential when addressed. In fact, the companies that can effectively navigate these harsh realities are poised to emerge as the leaders of tomorrow.

First and foremost, we must recognize that these challenges are not isolated issues but symptoms of a broader shift in the business ecosystem. The rules of the game have changed and continue to change at an unprecedented pace. Success in this new era requires a fundamental rethinking of how we create value, engage with stakeholders, and define success.

Consider the words of management guru Peter Drucker: "The greatest danger in times of turbulence is not the turbulence itself, but to act with yesterday's logic." This sentiment captures the core challenge facing established businesses today. The strategies and mindsets that brought success in the past may well be the very things holding companies back in the present.

Here are five key action steps to help business leaders navigate these harsh realities and position their organizations for sustainable success:

TEMPLATES

Embrace Purpose-Driven Leadership

Define and articulate a clear, compelling purpose for your organization that goes beyond profit. This purpose should serve as a North Star, guiding decision-making at all levels and fostering a sense of meaning and belonging among employees and customers.

Cultivate Agility & Adaptability

Review your operational model and consider implementing agile methodologies not just in product development, but across all aspects of your organization. This includes creating cross-functional teams, embracing iterative processes, and fostering a culture that values experimentation and learning from failure.

Prioritize Long-Term Value Creation

Develop a balanced scorecard that includes short-term financial metrics and long-term value creation indicators. Communicate this holistic view of success to all stakeholders, including shareholders, and align incentives accordingly.

Invest in Employee Growth and Well-being

Create personalized development plans for employees that align their growth with organizational needs. Implement programs that support mental health, work-life balance, and overall well-being. Let's not forget, engaged employees are your greatest asset in navigating turbulent times.

Foster Genuine Customer Partnerships

Move beyond transactional customer relationships. Implement systems and processes that allow for deep, ongoing engagement with customers. This could include co-creation initiatives, customer advisory boards, and personalized success programs.

Implementing these action steps requires courage, commitment, and a willingness to challenge the status quo. It may mean making difficult decisions in the short term for the sake of long-term viability. It will involve rethinking many aspects of how your business operates.

The potential rewards are immense. Companies that successfully navigate these harsh realities can achieve a level of resilience, innovation, and sustainable growth that sets them apart in an increasingly competitive landscape.

Take the transformation of Microsoft under Satya Nadella's leadership. By articulating a clear purpose ("to empower every person and every organization on the planet to achieve more"), fostering a growth mindset culture, and pivoting towards long-term value creation in cloud computing, Microsoft has reinvented itself and achieved remarkable success.

Or look at Patagonia, which has built a thriving business by putting purpose and sustainability at the core of everything they do. Their commitment to environmental stewardship and ethical business practices has not only created a loyal customer base but has also attracted top talent and driven innovation in sustainable product design.

These companies demonstrate that it's possible to thrive amidst the harsh realities we've discussed. They show that by aligning purpose, people, and long-term thinking, businesses can not only survive but flourish in today's complex environment.

The harsh realities we've explored are not just challenges to be overcome. They're opportunities for reinvention. They're a call to evolve, to innovate, and to redefine what business success looks like in the twenty-first century.

The path forward isn't easy, but it's necessary. It requires a new kind of leadership - one that balances vision with execution, purpose with profit, and short-term performance with long-term sustainability. It demands a commitment to continuous learning, adaptation, and growth.

As you reflect on these insights and action steps, I encourage you to take a hard look at your organization. Where do you see these harsh realities manifesting? What opportunities for transformation do they present? And most importantly, what will you do differently tomorrow to navigate these challenges?

The future belongs to those who can see beyond the harsh realities of today to the possibilities of tomorrow. It belongs to leaders who can inspire their teams, delight their customers, and create lasting value in a world of constant change.

You have the power to be one of those leaders. The journey starts now. Are you ready to embrace these harsh realities and turn them into your competitive advantage?

02

CHAPTER

Analyzing the Root Cause

Finding the Hidden Problems That Block Your Growth

In business leadership, being able to spot what's really holding your company back is like having a secret map. You might wonder why, despite your best efforts, your company seems stuck. The answer usually isn't what you see on the surface. It's the deep problems that hide from casual observation.

Take a software company that was struggling after early success. CEO Marten told me, "We were doing everything by the book - or so we thought. Our products were cutting-edge, our team was talented, but we couldn't break through to the next level." It wasn't until his team took a hard look at themselves that they found the cracks in their foundation.

This chapter is your guide to that process. We'll explore how to do root-cause analysis - a process that can change your company's trajectory. But fair warning: this isn't easy. It takes courage to look honestly at your company's weaknesses and wisdom to tell the difference between real causes and symptoms.

Peter Drucker said it best: "The most serious mistakes are not being made as a result of wrong answers. The truly dangerous thing is asking the wrong questions." In the following sections, we'll give you the right questions - the ones that will light up the path to sustainable growth and help you avoid the traps that catch 70% of tech companies.

The goal isn't only to find problems. It's to uncover opportunities. Each challenge you discover is a potential catalyst for innovation, a chance to improve your strategies and strengthen your company's core. By the end of this chapter, you'll have the tools to turn obstacles into stepping stones that push your company toward unprecedented success.

Building a Rock-Solid Foundation and Strategy

In the fast-moving tech world, a strong foundation isn't just important - it's everything. Imagine trying to build a skyscraper on shifting sand.

No matter how innovative your design or skilled your team, the structure will fail. Similarly, your company's core vision and the expertise of your leadership team form the bedrock all your future success will be built on.

Let's start with a basic question: What is your company's core vision? This isn't just about having a catchy mission statement on your office walls. It's about having a clear, compelling, and actionable purpose that resonates throughout every level of your organization. Your vision should be the North Star guiding all strategic decisions, from product development to market expansion.

Consider Neuwerk, a mid-sized IT firm from Hamburg, Germany that had been treading water for years. When new CEO Marcus took over, his first move was to look at the company's vision. "We realized our vision had become stale," Marcus says. "It no longer reflected the rapidly changing needs of our clients or the evolving technology landscape. We were trying to navigate the future using an outdated map."

Marcus brought his leadership team together for intensive strategy sessions. The goal wasn't merely to write a new vision statement but to deeply understand the company's unique value and how it could meet emerging market needs. This process revealed a critical gap: while the team was technically good, they lacked the strategic thinking needed to anticipate and capitalize on industry trends.

To fix this, Marcus used a two-part approach. First, he invested in executive education programs focused on strategic leadership in tech. Second, he brought in a diverse advisory board with experience in adjacent industries, providing fresh perspectives and challenging old assumptions. This external advisory board was initially planned to only serve for a few months until things stabilize. After three months Marcus decided to turn this short-term engagement into a permanent advisory team.

The results were transformative. Within eighteen months, Neuwerk had pivoted its service offerings, focusing on emerging technologies that aligned perfectly with their newly clarified vision. Revenue grew by 40%, and employee satisfaction scores hit an all-time high.

But vision alone isn't enough. You need to translate that vision into actionable strategy. This is where many companies fail, getting lost in the gap between aspiration and execution. Your strategy should be a living document, constantly evolving based on market feedback and internal capabilities.

Ask yourself: How often do we revisit and refine our strategy? Are we truly using the collective expertise of our leadership team, or are we falling into groupthink? Are we balancing short-term goals with long-term sustainability?

Strategy isn't only about setting goals - it's about making tough choices. As Harvard Business School professor Michael Porter emphasizes, "The essence of strategy is choosing what not to do." Your strategy should clearly state not just what you aim to achieve, but also what you're willing to give up in pursuit of your vision.

Setting up a strong strategic planning process is crucial. This could involve quarterly strategy reviews, annual off-site planning sessions, or adopting frameworks like OKRs (Objectives and Key Results) to ensure alignment between vision, strategy, and execution.

By strengthening your foundation and sharpening your strategic approach, you not only solve today's problems - you position your company to thrive in tomorrow's challenges. In the next section, we'll explore how this solid foundation can help you truly understand and serve your customers, setting the stage for sustainable growth.

Understanding Your Customers: Mastering Market Intelligence

In tech, understanding your customer isn't just a competitive advantage - it's the lifeblood of your business. Yet too often, companies operate on assumptions rather than insights, building products and services for imagined needs rather than real-world demands. Let's unravel this customer puzzle and explore how deep market intelligence can accelerate your growth.

I remember working with a startup some time ago. They had burned through millions in venture capital before realizing their fundamental error. "We were so excited about our technology that we forgot to talk to potential customers," admits former CTO Elena. Their sleek solution struggled to get their first customers while the company scrambled to understand why their "revolutionary" product wasn't selling.

This scenario raises a crucial question: Do we truly understand our customers, or are we just projecting our own excitement? The answer lies in rigorous, empathetic market research that goes beyond superficial surveys and focus groups.

Imagine you're an anthropologist studying a new culture. That's the level of curiosity and detail you should bring to understanding your customers. How do they operate? What are their pain points? What metrics define success in their world? What impact would solving a specific pain have, and who would benefit most? These aren't mere academic questions - they're the key to unlocking unprecedented value and loyalty.

I remember Neubasis, a B2B software provider that revolutionized its approach to product development. CEO Peter implemented a program where every employee, from developers to executives, spent two days a year shadowing customers. "It was eye-opening," Peter recalls. "We thought we were selling efficiency, but our customers were buying peace of mind. This insight reshaped our entire go-to-market strategy."

To truly understand your customers, ask these critical questions:

Are we relying on data and assumptions, or have we invested time in understanding our customers and what provides value?

Do we understand how they operate, how they generate revenue, and what they genuinely need?

Have we mapped out the goals and KPIs (key performance indictors) of the people involved in buying and using our products & services?

Do we have a clear understanding of how to efficiently and effectively reach our target customers?

In the age of information overload, making it easy for the right prospects to find you and do business with you is paramount. This is where your go-to-market model becomes crucial. It's not just about having a great product; it's about ensuring that product finds its way into the hands of who needs it most.

Consider implementing a Voice of Customer (VoC) program that systematically collects and analyzes customer feedback across multiple touchpoints. This isn't just about addressing complaints - it's about identifying unspoken needs and emerging trends that could inform your next big innovation.

Moreover, don't underestimate the power of predictive analytics. By using AI and machine learning, you can move beyond reactive customer service to proactive customer success. Imagine being able to anticipate your clients' needs before they even voice them - that's the power of advanced market intelligence.

But gathering data is only a starting point. The real magic happens when you validate data with real life customer interviews and transform that data into actionable insights. Create cross-functional teams that regularly analyze customer data, looking for patterns and anomalies that could signal new opportunities or looming threats. Validate your findings and assumptions by talking to your customers. Just relying on data might lead you in the wrong direction.

Your goal isn't just to satisfy customers - it's to create advocates. In the words of Amazon's Jeff Bezos, "We see our customers as invited guests to a party, and we are the hosts. It's our job every day to make every important aspect of the customer experience a little bit better."

By mastering market intelligence, you don't only improve your current offerings - you position your company to lead the next wave of innovation. In our next section, we'll explore how this customer-centric approach can be woven into the very fabric of your organization through clear roles, responsibilities, and goals.

Getting Clear: Defining Roles, Responsibilities, and Goals

In the complex machinery of a tech company, each part must not only fit perfectly but also understand its crucial role in the bigger picture. Yet in the frantic pace of innovation and market shifts, roles can blur, responsibilities can overlap, and goals can become as foggy as a San Francisco morning. Let's cut through this confusion and explore how crystal-clear clarity can supercharge your organization's performance.

I remember London based company DCPP, a promising software and services startup, found itself stuck in missed deadlines and department conflicts. Despite a team of brilliant minds, progress had ground to a halt. "It was like watching world-class musicians trying to play a symphony without a conductor or sheet music," recalls GM Ben. "Individually talented but collectively chaotic."

This scenario raises a critical question: Do we have a clear understanding and description of each role in our organization? It's not enough to have talented people; they need to know exactly where they fit in the grand scheme.

We implemented a transparency initiative. Every role in the company was carefully defined, not just in terms of responsibilities but in terms of its impact on the company's mission. "We created what we call 'Role Canvases,'" Ben explains. "These aren't just job descriptions; they're strategic blueprints that show how each position contributes to our overarching goals."

But clarity of roles is only the first step. The real power comes from aligning these roles with razor-sharp goals. Ask yourself: Is there a "number-one" goal for each role and person? Is this goal understood by each employee, and are they enabled and empowered to be successful in their role? Do we have the right people in the right roles?

Consider the OKR (Objectives and Key Results) framework popularized by Google. This isn't just a goal-setting exercise; it's a communication tool that ensures everyone is rowing in the same direction. When implemented correctly, OKRs can create a powerful sense of purpose and alignment throughout your organization.

Let me give you an example. A cloud platform company that was struggling with siloed departments and misaligned priorities. I worked with CTO George and introduced a modified OKR system where each employee's primary objective was directly tied to a company-wide goal. "The transformation was almost immediate," George notes. "Suddenly, our marketing team was talking to our engineers about how they could collaborate to improve user onboarding. It wasn't just about hitting individual targets anymore; it was about collective success."

Setting clear goals is a good starting point. On top, you need to empower your team to achieve them. This means providing the resources, authority, and support necessary for success. It's about creating an environment where your team doesn't just understand their roles but feels ownership over them. To achieve this, it is essential to have a clear vision that guides the way, an organization structure that supports daily operation, and an execution strategy that allows employees to contribute their talent to the maximum benefit for the company. We will focus on each of these areas individually later.

Implement regular "alignment check-ins" where team members can discuss how their individual goals contribute to the bigger picture. And where they can give feedback on what they need to be successful in their role. This isn't about micromanagement; it's about fostering a culture of collective responsibility and shared success. If your employees understand how their personal goals fit into the larger picture and if they are enabled and empowered, they will go the extra mile to achieve their goals.

Empowerment without accountability is chaos. Clear roles and goals should be accompanied by measurable metrics and regular reviews. These reviews shouldn't be feared; they should be seen as opportunities for growth and recalibration. They should provide an opportunity to learn and adopt.

As leadership expert John C. Maxwell puts it, "A leader is one who knows the way, goes the way, and shows the way." By providing crystal-clear direction, you don't just manage your team; you inspire them to reach heights they may have thought impossible.

Clarity in roles, responsibilities, and goals isn't only about organizational efficiency - it's about unleashing the full potential of your human capital.

When everyone knows their part in the symphony and can hear how it contributes to the overall masterpiece, that's when true organizational harmony is achieved.

Talent Matching: The Art of Getting People in the Right Roles

In the high-stakes world of technology, having the right people in the right roles isn't just important - it's the difference between stagnation and innovation, between being a market follower and a market leader. Yet too often, companies fall into the trap of square pegs in round holes, misaligning talent and hindering their potential for growth. Let's explore the nuanced art of talent matching - transforming your organization by optimizing your human capital.

I remember working with REGMBH, a German hardware and software company that was struggling to bring its groundbreaking technology to market. Despite a team of brilliant scientists and engineers, progress was painfully slow. CTO George had an epiphany during a late-night review session: "We had world-class researchers and product managers leading our commercialization efforts. We were setting everyone up for frustration and failure."

This realization prompts a crucial question: Are we clear on the type of person we need for each specific role? It's not just about qualifications on paper; it's about understanding the unique blend of skills, experience, and personality traits that will make someone thrive in a particular position. This requires a thorough review of the exact requirements for a specific role. It also needs to include how that specific role interfaces with other roles within and outside of your company. We will discuss this important topic in chapter 6.

I worked with George on a comprehensive talent audit, collaborating with external industrial psychologists to create detailed profiles for each key role in the organization. "We went beyond just listing required skills," he explains. "We defined the cognitive styles, work preferences, and even the cultural attributes that would lead to success in each position."

But identifying the ideal profile is only half the equation. The real challenge lies in consistently evaluating whether candidates or current employees possess these attributes. This is where many organizations fail, relying on gut feelings or outdated assessment methods. How many employees did you exchange hoping the next one will do a better job? How often did you just take a role description template from a shared drive? I have seen this so many times happening and to be honest, I have done it myself.

Consider implementing a multi-faceted evaluation process that goes beyond traditional interviews and resumes. This might include:

1. NLP or similar technologies to understand a candidate's characteristics and personality
2. Role-specific simulations to study behavior in team settings
3. Cultural fit assessments to ensure alignment with your organization's values
4. Peer interviews to gauge team dynamics and collaboration potential

The goal isn't to find perfect employees - they don't exist. It's about finding the right fit for each role and your organization as a whole.

I remember vividly a senior executive (let's call him Francesco) who interviewed me years ago for a general manager position. Francesco was a charismatic and friendly leader. We had a good exchange about their requirements for the role and about how I approach business. I felt quite good and the conversation was going well. At one point during the interview, he told me: "We are going to do a little role play now, and I apologize in advance because I might cause more pain than visiting your dentist."

I was getting nervous and my hands started to get sweaty. I accepted the challenge (what option did I have). When I was presenting my findings and solution, he was questioning my rationale behind my answers and showing me what I did not consider in my thought process. Francesco was right, this role play was painful and I felt like an idiot. While writing these words I can still feel the pain of that day in my body and my hands start sweating again.

What he explained later was that the role-play was not about finding the right solution (there wasn't a right solution anyways) but about how I would act under pressure, how I would respond to criticism and failure, and whether I was able to self-reflect quickly and take other points of view into account.

I learned a lot that day but the learning didn't come easily.

The above example unfortunately is very rare. Most companies don't put much effort into hiring, although they would argue they do. If you look at generic role descriptions, inconsistent interview workflows, and the lack of specific expertise of the people involved, you will probably agree there is room for improvement.

Talent optimization doesn't stop at hiring. It's an ongoing process of development and realignment. Regular skills assessments and career path discussions should be integral parts of your talent management strategy. This not only ensures you maximize the potential of your current team but also helps in retention by showing employees a clear path for growth within your organization.

Don't underestimate the power of cognitive diversity. In the fast-paced world of tech, having a team that approaches problems from different angles can be your secret weapon. As management guru Peter Drucker once said, "The best way to predict the future is to create it." By assembling a cognitively diverse team, you create an environment ripe for breakthrough innovations.

Implement regular "talent calibration" sessions where leaders across the organization come together to discuss the performance and potential of their team members. Involve an expert in the field of psychology or NLP in the process to get a wider perspective beyond a traditional business view. Hire an expert or use an external specialist with a background in psychology. This will be the best investment of your life. This isn't about shallow reviews; it's about ensuring every individual is in a position where they can make their maximum contribution to the organization. For poor performing employees ask yourself what might be the reason. Are they wrong in their role? Are they enabled to do what is expected? Are they motivated?

In the knowledge economy, your people are your most valuable asset. Do you treat the people topic like this? By mastering the art of talent matching - getting the right people in the right roles – you don't merely build a team; you craft the engine that will drive your organization's future success.

The North Star Principle: Aligning People and Goals

The North Star of a company is not a generic vision and mission statement that can be found on most company websites. The North Star is a vision that unites all people of a company to achieve a visionary goal and, if implemented well, guides all future decisions.

A true North Star vision is unique to your specific company and distinguishes it from any other company. It is a vision that is easy to remember and that employees can relate to and identify with. The North Star vision is the reason your company exists.

In a fast-paced world, a powerful North Star vision can guide your organization through the often-turbulent seas of the tech business. Yet most companies lack a strong North Star vision and just have an interchangeable vision and mission statement.

Without an inspiring North Star vision any bigger transformation initiative will fail.

I remember discussing the North Star topic with an international business process automation software provider. Their leadership team was convinced that their vision and mission statement that marketing crafted was good enough. I asked the team to randomly pick ten employees from different functions and ask them what they think the company's vision was. To their surprise, not a single one could state the exact vision or relate to a broader company vision.

Take the example of Google. Their North Star vision is: "To organize the world's information and make it universally accessible and useful."

One of the best North Star visions I ever came across is from a U.S.-based chain called Greyston Bakery. Their North Star vision is: "We don't hire people to bake brownies; we bake brownies to hire people." Every employee in the company is absolutely clear that the more brownies they bake, the more uneducated people will get a job. This unites everyone in the company to one goal.

Imagine you need to make a business decision. You ask one question: Does it help to bake more brownies and consequently hire more people? This is the level of clarity a true North Star vision should provide, and we will focus on this important topic in chapter 4.

Building an Efficient Organizational Structure

In the dynamic world of tech, your organizational structure is more than just boxes and lines on a chart - it's the very architecture of your success. The organizational structure dictates how people and teams work together. Yet many companies find themselves trapped in outdated hierarchies that slow down innovation and block agility.

Let's explore how to design an organizational structure that not only supports efficient collaboration but also centers around the evolving needs of your customers.

Many traditional companies have implemented some sort of matrix organizational model. Invented in the 1950s, this organizational style was built with the intention of giving maximum control and efficiency. While these models have worked well in stable markets over a long period, they don't allow for business agility that is required in today's fast-changing market conditions.

In reality, matrix-style organizations can become very siloed. My experience is that most matrix organizations are siloed. Each function is building its own silo with their own goals, KPIs, and success criteria. Cross-functional alignment often becomes difficult and slow, especially when conflicting KPIs have been established.

In today's fast-paced world, the crucial question is: Does our organizational structure support efficient collaboration and rapid response to market demands? Or is it built for maximum command and control?

In the last few years, younger companies have been built differently, with a focus on agility and shared ownership instead of focusing on top-down command and maximum control. Companies like Spotify have been leading this trend towards agile organizational models that are centered around customer needs and organized in cross-functional teams.

Another example is Amazon with their so-called "two pizza teams." These are groups of people small enough to be fed by two pizzas, five to ten people max.

One of my clients recently started a bold restructuring journey. They moved away from traditional functional silos towards a more fluid, orbit-like structure organized around customer segments and product lines. "We created 'Value Streams,'" their COO explains. "Each stream is a cross-functional team dedicated to delivering specific value to a particular customer segment."

This customer-centric approach to organizational design can be transformative. Consider implementing regular "structural health checks" where you assess how well your current structure serves your customers and supports your strategic goals. This isn't about constant reorganization, but rather about ensuring your structure remains aligned with your evolving business needs.

An efficient org structure also needs a robust execution system to turn that structure into results. Ask yourself: Are we tracking the right things to understand whether we're making progress and to find areas for improvement?

Best practice is implementing an Objectives and Key Results (OKR) system, popularized by tech giants like Google and Intel. This approach not only helps in setting and communicating goals but also in tracking progress and identifying bottlenecks in real-time.

The goal isn't to create a perfect, static structure - it's to design an organization that can learn, adapt, and evolve. As management theorist

Gary Hamel puts it, "The goal is to build an organization that's as nimble as change itself."

Implement regular "structural retrospectives" where teams across the organization come together to discuss how well the current structure is serving their needs and the needs of customers. This isn't about complaining; it's about continuously refining and optimizing your organizational design.

By mastering the art of organizational design and execution, you don't just improve efficiency - you create a responsive, adaptable organization capable of thriving in the face of rapid technological and market changes. When your structure aligns with your strategy and centers around customer value, that's when true organizational excellence is achieved.

Getting Your Technology Stack Right

In the digital world of tech, your technology stack isn't just a collection of tools - it's the backbone of your competitive advantage. Yet many organizations find themselves stuck with outdated systems or drowning in a sea of mismatched technologies. Let's explore the art of crafting a technology stack that doesn't just support your goals but actively pushes you toward them.

Most companies I worked with have a focus on consolidating systems with the goal to save cost and to have all data in a limited set of applications. They focus on internal needs rather than customer requirements. Best-in-class companies look at systems from a customer perspective and select the technology that serves best for any given customer or internal interaction and task.

Think of Amazon when they were just an online bookstore. When they started their journey to launch Amazon Web Services (AWS), they did not limit themselves to the tech stack that they had in place but looked at what technology would be best to provide for excellent user experience for their new business segment. Imagine how they would have limited themselves if they only stuck to their existing technology stack made for selling books.

I remember working for a software company that had acquired a young Vancouver based startup company. That startup company had developed a best-in-class inbound marketing engine using a blend of different marketing automation tools with custom programming. They had spent a lot of time and money on this system, but it paid off by delivering stellar results.

Shortly after the acquisition, the CMO of the acquiring company decided to abandon this custom-built marketing engine in favor of moving toward central corporate systems. The effects of this move were disheartening. Lead inflow dried up, and cost per lead increased ten times within weeks. To make things worse, the leading researcher of the custom marketing engine was frustrated and left the company after a month.

These stories raise a crucial question: Does the technology we use truly support us in driving towards our goals? How can technology improve customer experience, and which solutions would work best? Are our technology decisions driven by internal needs or are they customer centric? Who understand the requirements of a solution best and are they involved in the decision-making process?

A process of technological introspection can be transformative. Consider implementing a regular "tech stack health check" where you assess the efficiency and effectiveness of each component in your technology ecosystem. This isn't about chasing the latest trends but about ensuring your tools align with your strategic objectives and empower your team to perform at their best.

But having the right technology is only half the battle. You also need the right expertise to leverage it effectively. Ask yourself: Do we have the right experts in place to understand what technology would support each function, team, and process towards our vision and goals?

Consider creating "technology champions" within each department - individuals who stay current with technological advancements in their area and serve as a bridge between IT and business functions. This ensures that technology decisions are driven by real business needs, not just IT imperatives.

The goal isn't to have the most advanced technology stack - it's to have the most effective one for your specific needs and goals. As tech visionary Steve Jobs once said, "It's not about pop culture, and it's not about fooling people, and it's not about convincing people that they want something they don't. We figure out what we want. And I think we're pretty good at having the right discipline to think through whether a lot of other people are going to want it, too."

Implement regular "tech horizon scanning" sessions where your technology champions and business leaders come together to explore emerging technologies and their potential impact on your industry. This isn't about chasing every shiny new tool; it's about staying ahead of the curve and identifying technologies that could give you a significant competitive edge. With the rapid evolution of AI this is more important than ever. I have seen large companies rolling out company wide AI tools hoping to increase efficiency. Reality shows the impact of this approach is minimal. Best in class companies identify specific processes that they want to optimize with the help of AI. Then they evaluate which solution would be best for a specific process and what the new AI improved process would look like. Only then and after evaluating risk versus opportunity and cost they would start implementing.

By mastering the art of technology stack optimization, you don't just improve efficiency - you create a foundation for innovation and growth. When your technology aligns perfectly with your strategy and empowers your team, that's when true digital transformation is achieved.

From Analysis to Action

As we conclude, it's crucial to remember that analysis without action is just an academic exercise. The journey we've taken is not just about identifying problems. It's about seizing opportunities, catalyzing growth, and transforming your organization into an agile, innovative powerhouse in the tech landscape.

The stories we've shared serve as a powerful reminder: the insights you've gained are not meant to gather dust in a report. They are your blueprint for revolutionary change. As management guru Peter Drucker wisely noted, "Plans are only good intentions unless they immediately degenerate into hard work."

Here are five actionable steps to analyze the current state:

Review your Vision and Mission

Take an honest look at your current vision and mission statement (and North Star if your company has one). Do they inspire you? Are they unique to your company or? Write down the current version and take notes on your thought. Ask 10 people within your organization whether they know the vision and mission statement. Ask them what they think your companies' vision is and what inspires them.

Check your Goals vs. Reality

Reflect on what the big goals for the last 12 months were and what reality looks like. Which goals have been achieved, partially or in full? Which goals have been completely missed? Which Initiatives got postponed or canceled? Where are your KPIs compared to plan? What are the most important KPIs that you track and are they leading or lagging KPIs? Take notes of your findings.

Map your Organization Structure

Review how your company is organized. Take a look at the current org chart and how initiatives and processes run through the organization. Write down where decisions are made, where hand offs happen and how alignment is organized. Also take a look at your organization from a customer perspective. To what extent is your organization designed towards customer needs versus internal requirements? Reflect on whether the current design is built for command and maximum control or whether it is optimized for maximum speed, autonomy and agility.

Identify your Top Customers

Make a list of your top ten customers. These should be the customers that are generating the biggest value out of using your solutions or services. Capture company size, industry, location and solutions they use. Gather the key contacts within these customers. These should include key users, decision makers, influencers and top management. We will need this information in Chapter 5 to refine your ideal customer profile.

Study your Role Descriptions

Review job descriptions of the main functions within your organization. Also take a look at your leadership role descriptions. Write down what required skills are listed. Note whether there is a description of personality, characteristics and personal traits. What personality type is required for the role. Take a look at the description of the typical tasks and success criteria for that specific role. Does it show how the role fits into organizational structure and how it interfaces with other functions? Does it mention how that role contributes to the overall creation of value? We will work on talent assessment and hiring in chapter six.

Start a Tech Stack Audit

Conduct a comprehensive review of your current technology infrastructure. Identify gaps, redundancies, and opportunities for improvement. Review who owns and influences your tech stack to support your strategic goals. Evaluate which elements are serving your customers' needs versus your internal requirements. Is technical expertise centralized in IT or embedded in functional business teams? Technology should be an enabler, not a hindrance.

TEMPLATES

As you start this transformative journey, remember that change is not a destination - it's an ongoing process. The tech sector will continue to evolve, and so must your organization. The tools and insights you've gained are not just for solving today's problems; they're for building a culture of continuous improvement and adaptation.

In the words of organizational theorist Rosabeth Moss Kanter, "The most effective leaders look for ways to win small victories to motivate their people and maintain momentum." Each step you take, each improvement you make, is a victory that propels you forward.

You stand at the threshold of extraordinary potential. The challenges you've identified are not obstacles; they're opportunities waiting to be seized. By addressing the root causes, you don't just solve problems. You lay the groundwork for unprecedented growth, innovation, and success.

The future of your organization is in your hands. Armed with these insights and action steps, you have the power to transform challenges into triumphs, to turn potential into performance. The journey of a thousand miles begins with a single step. Take that step today, and watch as your organization soars to new heights in the dynamic world of technology.

Key Takeaways

Let's recap the essential insights that will serve as your roadmap for sustainable growth and industry leadership:

Foundation and Strategy:

The importance of a clear, compelling vision that guides all strategic decisions

Translating vision into actionable strategy, constantly evolving based on market feedback and internal capabilities

Customer Understanding:

The critical need for deep, empathetic market research beyond superficial surveys and data

Implementing Voice of Customer programs and using predictive analytics for proactive customer success

Roles, Responsibilities, and Goals:

The necessity of clearly defined roles and their impact on the company's mission

Aligning individual goals with company-wide objectives using frameworks like OKRs

Talent Alignment:

The art of matching people to roles based on skills, experience, and personality traits

Implementing multi-faceted evaluation processes and ongoing talent development strategies

Organizational Structure:

Designing structures that support efficient collaboration and center around customer needs

The concept of 'Value Streams' and cross-functional teams for more fluid, responsive organizations

Technology Stack:

The critical role of a well-aligned technology stack in driving innovation and competitive advantage

Regular 'Tech Stack Health Checks' and the importance of having the right expertise to leverage technology effectively

Identifying root causes is a crucial first step building the basis for change. The real value comes from translating these insights into actionable strategies that drive continuous improvement and adaptation in the fast-paced technology industry.

03

CHAPTER

Building a Solid Business Foundation

Back in Boston for a quarterly meeting. The conference room went quiet as Catherine, CEO of Teamworx, slid a document across the table. Her co-founder, Karim, watched as I opened what would become one of the most impressive business documents I'd seen in two decades of business leadership.

"This," Catherine said quietly, "is why we're growing 340% faster than our closest competitor."

What I saw wasn't just another business plan collecting dust on a shelf. This was a living company playbook – eighty-five pages of crystallized wisdom that had transformed two MIT graduates with a promising algorithm into leaders of a $200 million business in just four years.

When I first met Catherine and Karim about five years ago, I was truly impressed, and they still inspire my daily work. Two passionate business leaders with complementing expertise in different fields. Catherine, a powerhouse in people, culture, and organizational design with deep knowledge in their target market. Karim, a mastermind in system design, psychology, and marketing.

Their growth defied industry norms. While most SaaS companies struggle to maintain 20 to 30% annual growth, Teamworx was sustaining triple-digit expansion without the typical growing pains. No revolving door of executives. No culture problems. No customer churn spikes.

The secret, they explained, wasn't just their revolutionary approach to predictive analytics - it was their foundational architecture.

"Most companies build the plane while flying it," Catherine explained. "We decided to engineer the blueprint first."

As I studied their playbook, I discovered something remarkable. This wasn't just documentation - it was strategic DNA. Every page reflected months of deliberate thought about who they were, where they were going, and how they'd get there. They'd defined not only their North Star vision but created complementary product and people visions that aligned like planets around a common center.

The organizational structure section revealed another layer of sophistication. Unlike typical org charts that look like family trees, theirs looked like a jazz ensemble - structured enough for harmony, flexible enough for improvisation. Each role came with detailed personality profiles and skill requirements, creating what Catherine called "intentional complementarity."

Here's what stunned me most: when I interviewed fifteen employees across different departments and seniority levels, their answers aligned with frightening precision. Ask anyone about the company's North Star and you'd get virtually identical responses. Question them about their role's contribution to the larger mission and they'd explain it with the clarity of a company spokesperson. Ask them how they feel about working for Teamworks and they'd express gratitude and fun. People also reported feeling appreciated. Many stated that they feel supported and that they learned a lot.

This wasn't corporate brainwashing - it was authentic alignment.

Research from Harvard Business Review validates what Catherine and Karim discovered intuitively: the highest-performing executive teams invest 54% more time in setting initial direction, developing their unique vision, and turning it into clear, tangible objectives before moving to action. They then spend an additional 25% more time focusing on the practical aspects - establishing financial and operational metrics, connecting objectives with strategy, assigning resources, and reviewing key indicators.

As Alexander Graham Bell wisely observed: "Before anything else, preparation is the key to success."

The difference between companies that scale gracefully and those that stumble isn't talent, market conditions, or even product superiority. It's foundation. The companies that thrive have invested in the invisible architecture that supports everything visible - the strategic frameworks, cultural DNA, and operational systems that transform good intentions into sustainable results.

Think of your business foundation as the root system of a redwood tree. What you see above ground - the revenue, the team, the market presence - represents only a fraction of the total structure. Below the surface lies an intricate network of interconnected systems that determine whether your organization will weather storms or topple at the first strong wind.

Building this foundation isn't glamorous work. It requires patience in an impatient world, depth in a culture obsessed with surface metrics, and long-term thinking in an environment that rewards quarterly results. Yet it's precisely this foundational work that separates the companies that experience sustainable growth from those that experience temporary success followed by inevitable plateau or decline.

The following eight elements represent the core components of the "exponential foundation" - the strategic architecture that enables companies not just to grow but to scale exponentially while maintaining their essential character and operational excellence.

Setting Up a Diverse Strategy Team

Envision this scenario: you're assembling an elite special forces unit for the most critical mission of your career. Would you choose five versions of yourself, or would you deliberately seek complementary skills, diverse perspectives, and personalities that create synergy rather than redundancy?

Most CEOs unconsciously opt for the first approach when building their strategy teams. They gravitate toward people who think like them, share similar backgrounds, and validate their existing viewpoints. It's comfortable. It's predictable. And it's strategic suicide.

The companies that achieve exponential growth understand a fundamental truth: diversity isn't just a nice-to-have cultural value - it's competitive advantage in human form. When Canadian tech entrepreneur Rebecca was building her healthcare software platform, she could have surrounded herself with fellow engineers who spoke her technical language. Instead, she made a counterintuitive choice that would define her company's trajectory.

"I covered product and people because those were my natural strengths," Catherine explained when I interviewed her about Teamwork's remarkable growth story. "But I knew my blind spots would kill us if I didn't address them systematically."

So, she assembled what she called her "cognitive diversity council" - brilliant minds from psychology, mathematics, finance, and behavioral economics. Each brought not just different expertise but fundamentally different ways of processing information and solving problems. The mathematician saw patterns in user behavior that the psychologist missed. The finance expert identified revenue opportunities that the engineer overlooked. The behavioral economist predicted market reactions that surprised everyone else.

Here's the crucial part: Catherine never compromised on personality fit. Technical brilliance without emotional intelligence creates dysfunction. Diverse thinking without collaborative chemistry produces conflict rather than innovation. She spent six months interviewing candidates not just for their professional qualifications but for their ability to disagree respectfully, adapt quickly, and maintain curiosity even when challenged.

The result? Teamwork's strategy team became legendary within their industry. While competitors struggled with departmental silos and groupthink, Catherine's team generated breakthrough insights by combining perspectives that had never intersected before. Their ability to spot opportunities and anticipate challenges gave them an eighteen-month competitive advantage in a rapidly evolving market.

This approach requires "strategic vulnerability" - the courage to surround yourself with people who are smarter than you in specific areas, who will challenge your assumptions, and who won't simply execute your vision but will actively improve it. It means hiring for complementary strengths rather than comfortable similarities.

The best strategy teams operate like high-performance racing crews. Each member has a specialized role, but they all work toward the same finish line. The pit crew chief doesn't need to be the fastest driver, but they need to orchestrate flawless coordination under pressure. The tire specialist doesn't need to understand aerodynamics, but they need to execute their piece perfectly while trusting others to handle theirs.

Your strategy team's diversity should span four critical dimensions: cognitive diversity (different ways of thinking and problem-solving), experiential diversity (varied professional and life backgrounds), functional diversity (complementary skill sets and expertise areas), and personality diversity (different behavioral styles and communication preferences that create healthy tension rather than destructive conflict).

When you get this combination right, something remarkable happens. Your team begins to generate solutions no individual member could have conceived alone. They start to anticipate market shifts that catch competitors off-guard. They develop strategies that are simultaneously bold and practical, innovative and executable.

The investment in building this kind of team pays exponential dividends because every major decision benefits from multiple perspectives, every blind spot gets illuminated by someone else's strength, and every challenge becomes an opportunity for collective intelligence to emerge.

Developing a North Star Vision

What happens when you ask employees throughout your organization to recite your company's vision statement? If you're like most CEOs, you'll witness an uncomfortable comedy of errors - stammering, confused looks, and responses that sound like they're reading from different scripts entirely.

Now imagine walking through Greyston Bakery's production facility in Yonkers, New York. Ask any employee, from the newest hire to the seasoned baker, about their company's mission, and you'll get the same response: "We don't hire people to bake brownies; we bake brownies to hire people." It's not just memorized - it's internalized. Every decision, every policy, every hiring choice reflects this North Star principle of providing employment opportunities for people facing barriers to traditional employment.

This isn't corporate sloganeering. It's strategic DNA made manifest.

A true North Star vision transcends the typical mission statement that sounds impressive in boardrooms but means nothing to the people doing the actual work. It becomes the gravitational force that aligns every decision, every resource allocation, and every cultural norm around a shared understanding of purpose.

When I worked with TechServe Solutions, their original vision statement was forgettable corporate-speak: "To be the leading provider of innovative technology solutions that drive business transformation." Technically accurate. Strategically useless. It could have described ten thousand other companies. Employees were not inspired and even the CEO was not really excited.

We spent three months working with their leadership team to uncover their authentic North Star. Through customer interviews, employee surveys, and deep reflection on their unique value proposition, we discovered something powerful: TechServe didn't just implement software - they liberated human potential by automating soul-crushing repetitive work, freeing people to do what only humans can do brilliantly.

Their refined North Star became: "We rescue human genius from boring work." Suddenly, every project had meaning. Customer success wasn't just about technical implementation - it was about measuring how many hours of human creativity they'd unlocked. Employee satisfaction wasn't just about perks and pay - it was about contributing to human flourishing. Marketing wasn't just about features and benefits - it was about telling stories of transformation.

The most powerful North Star visions share three characteristics: they're emotionally resonant (people feel something when they hear it), they're actionably specific (they guide decision-making), and they're authentically unique (they couldn't describe any other organization).

Consider how Southwest Airlines' North Star of "democratizing the skies" guided every operational decision. It explained why they chose secondary airports (lower costs meant lower fares), why they maintained a single aircraft type (operational efficiency supported affordability), and why they hired for attitude over experience (cultural fit was essential for their mission of making flying accessible and enjoyable for everyone).

Your North Star should answer the question: "When we're successful, how is the world different?" Not "What do we sell?" or "How do we make money?" but "What change do we create that wouldn't exist without us?"

This requires brutal honesty about your organization's unique contribution. Most companies exist to make money. But the ones that achieve sustainable exponential growth exist to make money by creating something valuable that didn't exist before - whether that's democratizing access, unleashing human potential, solving previously unsolvable problems, or connecting people in meaningful ways.

The process of discovering your authentic North Star often reveals uncomfortable truths about the gap between your stated values and your actual behavior. That's the point. A genuine North Star creates productive tension that pulls your organization toward its highest potential rather than allowing it to drift toward mediocrity.

Developing the Ideal Customer Profile and Buyer Personas

Here's a question that makes most executives think: Would you rather have a thousand customers who tolerate your solution or a hundred customers who can't imagine their business without it?

The instinctive answer is obvious, yet most companies spend their energy chasing the first scenario. They cast wide nets, hoping to capture anyone willing to pay, and wonder why their conversion rates remain stubbornly low and their customer lifetime value disappoints quarter after quarter.

The breakthrough comes when you realize that your ideal customer isn't the customer you wish to have - it's the customer you can provide extraordinary value to. This distinction changes everything.

I learned this lesson when working with CloudSync, a promising startup whose founders were brilliant technologists but struggled with a frustrating paradox. Their solution was genuinely innovative, their team was exceptional, and their market opportunity was enormous. Yet their inbound conversion rates hovered around 2%, and their outbound efforts generated more frustration than revenue.

"Tell me about your ideal customer," I asked during our first strategy session.

The CEO launched into a detailed description of Fortune 500 companies with complex IT infrastructures, substantial budgets, and urgent need for data synchronization solutions. On paper, it sounded perfect.

"Now tell me about your three happiest customers," I continued.

As we analyzed their most successful implementations, a different pattern emerged. Their true sweet spot wasn't massive enterprises - it was mid-market companies with distributed teams, specific compliance requirements, and previous bad experiences with enterprise software vendors. These customers valued CloudSync's agility, responsiveness, and ability to implement quickly without months of bureaucratic overhead.

We spent the next two months conducting in-depth interviews with existing customers, lost prospects, and target personas within their actual ideal customer profile. The insights transformed their entire go-to-market approach.

We discovered that the buying committee typically included four distinct personas: the IT director (who evaluated technical requirements), the operations VP (who assessed business impact), the CFO (who scrutinized cost-benefit analysis), and the CEO (who made final decisions based on strategic alignment). Each persona had different priorities, communication preferences, and decision-making criteria.

The IT director cared about integration complexity and security protocols. The operations VP focused on productivity gains and user adoption rates. The CFO wanted clear ROI projections and total cost of ownership calculations. The CEO needed to understand competitive advantage and long-term strategic value.

Armed with these insights, CloudSync redesigned their entire customer acquisition approach. They created persona-specific content that addressed each stakeholder's unique concerns. They developed sales processes that acknowledged the complex decision-making dynamics within their target accounts. They trained their team to speak different languages depending on their audience.

The results were dramatic. Within six months, their inbound conversion rates quadrupled to 8.3%. Their outbound success rate more than doubled. Even more importantly, their customer satisfaction scores increased significantly because they were now serving clients who truly valued their unique capabilities.

This transformation required abandoning the comfortable illusion that "everyone could be a customer" and embracing the uncomfortable truth that deep specialization creates sustainable competitive advantage. When you try to serve everyone, you serve no one exceptionally well. When you focus intensely on serving your ideal customer profile, you create experiences so valuable that competitors become irrelevant.

The key insight: your ideal customer profile isn't just a marketing exercise - it's a strategic filter that should influence product development, hiring decisions, partnership opportunities, and resource allocation. Every major business decision should pass the test: "Does this help us serve our ideal customers more effectively?"

Crafting a Go-to-Market Strategy

Imagine you're a master locksmith with the perfect key, but you're trying to open every door in the building instead of finding the specific lock it was designed for. That's exactly what happens when companies develop brilliant solutions but deploy misaligned go-to-market strategies.

The most elegant product in the world becomes irrelevant if it can't reach the people who need it most through channels they trust at moments when they're ready to act.

This reality hit home when I met Mark, CEO of FinanceFlow, during what he later described as his company's "darkest hour." His team had built an exceptional financial management platform specifically designed for CFOs at mid-market companies. The solution was sophisticated enough to handle complex requirements but simple enough to implement without massive consulting engagements.

"We had a product that CFOs loved," Mark explained, his frustration still evident months later. "Our demos were phenomenal. Customer satisfaction was through the roof. But we were bleeding cash because we couldn't efficiently get in front of the right people."

Their go-to-market strategy seemed logical on the surface: hire enterprise sales reps to make direct calls to CFOs at target companies. The problem? CFOs at mid-market companies don't have time for cold calls from unknown vendors. They're overwhelmed with operational responsibilities and suspicious of solutions that promise to solve problems they've learned to manage through workarounds.

The mismatch between their brilliant solution and their go-to-market approach was killing their growth trajectory.

During our strategy sessions, we mapped out five potential go-to-market models: Direct Sales, Inside Sales, Web-Based Self-Service, Reseller Channels, and Partner-Influenced Sales. Each model has distinct advantages depending on four critical variables: product complexity, ideal customer profile, buying committee dynamics, and price-to-margin ratios.

For FinanceFlow, direct sales made sense for enterprise deals but was economically inefficient for their mid-market focus. Their solution required explanation but wasn't complex enough to justify expensive sales cycles. Their buying persona (the CFO) was accessible but preferred trusted referrals over cold outreach.

The breakthrough came when we identified an adjacent technology ecosystem where their ideal customers were already making purchasing decisions: accounting software platforms. CFOs who needed sophisticated financial management solutions were already buying, implementing, and relying on these platforms.

We developed what became known as the "adjacent authority strategy." Instead of competing for attention in a crowded marketplace, FinanceFlow positioned itself as the natural evolution for companies that had outgrown their basic accounting software but weren't ready for enterprise-level complexity.

They systematically mapped resellers of complementary accounting technologies - consultants, implementation specialists, and software advisors who already had relationships with their ideal customer profile. These partners understood the pain points, spoke the language, and had earned the trust that FinanceFlow was trying to build from scratch.

The transformation was remarkable. Instead of cold-calling skeptical CFOs, they were being introduced by trusted advisors who could articulate the business case in language that resonated. Their sales cycles shortened by 40% because prospects came pre-qualified and pre-educated. Their cost of customer acquisition dropped by 60% while their close rates increased dramatically.

Within eighteen months, FinanceFlow's revenue grew 320% while their sales team actually decreased. They had discovered the exponential power of channel alignment - finding the path of least resistance between their solution and their ideal customers' decision-making process.

The lesson extends beyond software companies. Whether you're selling consulting services, physical products, or digital solutions, your go-to-market strategy should flow like water finding the most efficient route downhill, not like a battering ram trying to break through the strongest barriers.

Shaping an Agile Organization Structure

Walk into most corporate headquarters and you'll see something that would make a 1970s MBA proud: org charts that look like family trees, with clear hierarchical lines stretching from the CEO down through layers of management to individual contributors. It's orderly. It's predictable. And in today's business environment, it's organizational suicide.

The matrix organization structure, pioneered in the 1950s and widely adopted in the 1970s, was designed for a world where change happened slowly enough for bureaucracy to keep pace. Companies could afford vertical silos because markets were stable, customer expectations evolved gradually, and competitive threats emerged predictably.

That world no longer exists.

I witnessed this reality firsthand while consulting for a $50 million software company that had grown successful using traditional organizational principles. Their structure featured distinct vertical functions - global sales, global marketing, global product development - with matrix connections intended to enable cross-functional collaboration.

On paper, it looked sophisticated. In practice, it was dysfunctional.

When a major client requested a customized integration that required sales, marketing, and product development coordination, the process took four months to complete. Not because the work was complex - the actual development took three weeks. But because getting alignment across the vertical functions required sixteen meetings, seven approval cycles, and countless emails trying to reconcile conflicting KPIs and priorities.

Meanwhile, their competitor delivered a similar solution in six weeks using what they called "mission-based pods" - autonomous teams with end-to-end responsibility for specific customer outcomes.

The global VP of Implementation crystallized the problem during one particularly frustrating client escalation: "I'm measured solely on my team's utilization rates. Customer satisfaction isn't part of my scorecard, so I prioritize keeping my consultants busy with paid engagements over solving client problems quickly." While sales was asking him to hire more people he was struggling to even keep the current amount of people.

This is the matrix organization's fatal flaw: when vertical functions optimize for their own metrics rather than shared outcomes, the organization becomes internally focused rather than customer-obsessed. Silos emerge not by accident but by design, because the incentive structure rewards departmental performance over collaborative results.

The solution isn't abandoning structure - it's evolving to "jazz ensemble architecture." Like a jazz band, you need both structure and improvisation. The rhythm section provides the foundational beat (core systems and processes), but individual musicians have the freedom to solo when the music demands it (autonomous decision-making within defined parameters).

Companies leading this transition are organizing around outcomes rather than functions. Instead of separate sales, marketing, and customer success departments, they create customer experience pods with representatives from each discipline working toward shared metrics: customer lifetime value, net promoter score, customer achieved value, and revenue growth within specific market segments.

This shift requires fundamental changes in how you think about leadership, accountability, and resource allocation. Traditional managers become coaches who develop talent and remove obstacles rather than controlling workflow. Individual contributors gain broader responsibility and decision-making authority. Success gets measured by team outcomes rather than individual activities.

The benefits compound quickly. Decision cycles accelerate because fewer approvals are required. Innovation increases because diverse perspectives collaborate daily rather than occasionally. Customer satisfaction improves because entire teams focus on solving problems rather than completing tasks within departmental boundaries.

Most importantly, agile organization structures create what resilience researchers call "adaptive capacity" - the ability to respond effectively to unexpected challenges and opportunities. When the next market disruption arrives, you won't need months to realign your organization. Your teams will adapt organically because they're already structured around outcomes rather than processes.

Defining an Execution System

Strategy without execution is hallucination. Execution without strategy is chaos. The companies that achieve sustainable exponential growth master the art of translating ambitious visions into measurable progress through systematic execution frameworks.

To illustrate: research by Harvard Business School shows that 70% of strategic initiatives fail not because of poor strategy but because of poor execution. The gap between intention and implementation destroys more promising companies than market downturns, competitive threats, or technological disruption combined.

This execution gap explains why some of the world's most successful companies - Google, Intel, LinkedIn, Spotify - have embraced a deceptively simple framework that transforms strategic ambiguity into operational clarity: Objectives and Key Results or OKRs.

When John Doerr introduced OKRs to Google's founders in 1999, the company had forty employees and ambitious dreams. Today, Alphabet uses the same framework to coordinate hundreds of thousands of employees across dozens of countries and countless product lines. The system scales because it solves execution's fundamental challenge: ensuring everyone understands not just what they're supposed to do but why it matters and how success will be measured.

I observed this power firsthand while working with a rapidly growing supply chain software company. Their CEO, Maria, was frustrated by what she called "strategic drift" - the tendency for quarterly goals to evolve into wishful thinking rather than driving concrete results.

"We'd set aggressive targets in January," Maria explained, "and by March, everyone was working hard on important things that had nothing to do with our original objectives. We were busy but not effective."

We implemented OKRs - starting with the company's annual objectives, then focusing down through quarterly key results, team objectives, and individual contributions. Each level maintained clear line-of-sight to the level above while allowing autonomy in determining how to achieve results.

The transformation was immediate and measurable. Within one quarter, their execution velocity increased by 45%. Projects that previously took six months to complete were finishing in four months. More importantly, the quality of decision-making improved because every choice could be evaluated against clearly defined success criteria.

Here's what made the difference: they didn't just implement OKRs as a reporting mechanism - they embedded them into their organizational rhythm. Every Monday morning, teams shared progress updates. Every month, departments presented key results to the broader organization. Every quarter, the entire company participated in retrospectives that captured learnings and informed the next cycle's objectives.

This created what behavioral psychologists call a "feedback-rich environment" - a culture where progress becomes visible, obstacles surface quickly, and course corrections happen continuously rather than waiting for annual reviews or crisis moments.

The most powerful aspect of systematic execution isn't the framework itself - it's the organizational learning that emerges from consistent measurement and reflection. Teams develop pattern recognition about what works, what doesn't, and why. They become skilled at setting stretch goals that inspire exceptional performance without creating unrealistic expectations.

Companies that master execution systems discover something remarkable: they can pursue more ambitious strategies because they have confidence in their ability to translate vision into reality. They take calculated risks that competitors avoid because they know they'll detect problems early and adapt quickly.

Your execution system becomes your competitive advantage when it enables your organization to move faster, learn continuously, and maintain alignment even as you scale.

Defining Core Functions and Putting the Right People in Place

What if the most important hiring decision you make isn't about finding the smartest person in the room but about finding the person whose natural strengths perfectly complement your team's existing capabilities and whose weaknesses are covered by others' strengths?

This question challenges the conventional wisdom that dominates most hiring processes. We post job descriptions that read like superhero requirements - expecting candidates to be strategic visionaries and detail-oriented executors, empathetic coaches and decisive leaders, innovative thinkers and reliable operators, all wrapped into one impossible package. Let's be clear here, that candidate doesn't exist. And that profile is not even required. It just shows that you are not clear on the role requirements or that you haven't done a good enough job in describing what you really need for a specific role.

The reality is simpler and more powerful: exceptional teams are built through intentional complementarity, not individual perfection.

I learned this lesson while analyzing why certain executive teams consistently outperformed their peers. The pattern wasn't what you'd expect. The highest-performing teams didn't have the most individually brilliant members - they had members whose strengths and working styles created synergistic combinations that multiplied collective capability.

Take the leadership team at Katapult Systems, a software company that grew from startup to $100 million in revenue faster than any competitor in their space. Their success wasn't driven by hiring the most experienced cybersecurity executives available. Instead, they assembled what CEO Jennifer called her "cognitive puzzle" - five people whose thinking styles fit together like interlocking pieces.

Jennifer herself was a big-picture strategist who could see market opportunities eighteen months before competitors. Her CTO, Robert, was a systems thinker who excelled at translating vision into technical architecture. Their VP of Sales, Alex, was a relationship builder who could navigate complex enterprise sales cycles. The CFO, Lisa, was an analytical optimizer who found efficiency opportunities others missed. Their VP of People, Marcus, was an empathetic developer who could spot talent and build culture.

None of them could have built Katapult alone. Together, they created something exponentially more powerful than the sum of their individual capabilities.

"The magic happened in our weekly leadership meetings," Jennifer reflected. "Robert would identify technical constraints I hadn't considered. Alex would explain customer realities that changed our product roadmap. Lisa would find the financial models that made ambitious plans feasible. Marcus would anticipate the cultural implications of strategic decisions. Every major decision became better because it was filtered through five different types of intelligence."

This approach requires abandoning the comfortable myth that great leaders are equally strong in all dimensions. Instead, it demands honest self-assessment about your natural strengths and deliberate recruitment of people whose strengths cover your developmental areas.

The process starts with mapping your organization's critical functions - not just departmental responsibilities but the essential capabilities that drive success in your specific market. Then you identify the thinking styles, personality traits, and natural strengths required for each function to excel.

For example, your head of product development might need to be highly creative and comfortable with ambiguity, while your head of operations might need to be detail-oriented and process-focused. Your sales leader might thrive on relationship building and competitive pressure, while your finance leader might excel at pattern recognition and risk assessment.

The goal isn't finding people who can do everything adequately - it's finding people who can do specific things exceptionally well while collaborating effectively with teammates who excel in different areas.

High-performing teams also share three behavioral characteristics: they challenge each other respectfully (no one's ideas go unexamined), they support each other's success (individual achievement serves team objectives), and they maintain collective accountability (everyone owns team results, not just their functional area).

When you get this combination right, you create what organizational psychologists call "psychological safety with high standards" - an environment where people feel safe to take risks, admit mistakes, and ask for help, while maintaining relentless focus on exceptional performance.

Shift from PROJECT to PRODUCT

Here's a scenario that plays out in countless organizations: a brilliant idea emerges during a strategy session. Excitement builds. Resources get allocated. A project team forms with a clear timeline, defined deliverables, and specific budget. Everyone works intensely toward the launch date. The project completes successfully. The team disbands. Six months later, the initiative has quietly died from neglect, and everyone wonders why their investment didn't generate the expected returns.

This is the hidden cost of project-thinking in a product world.

The traditional project-centered model made sense when business change happened slowly and solutions could be built, deployed, and left to operate independently. But in today's environment - where customer expectations evolve continuously, competitive threats emerge overnight, and technology capabilities advance monthly rather than yearly - the project mindset becomes a competitive liability.

A 2018 Gartner survey revealed that 85% of companies prefer a product-centric model, and that percentage has undoubtedly increased as digital transformation accelerated through the pandemic and beyond. The companies making this transition aren't just changing their organizational charts - they're fundamentally reimagining how work gets done and value gets created.

I witnessed this transformation when working with StreamLink, where CEO Michael was frustrated. His company would invest significant resources developing new capabilities, celebrate successful launches, then watch as promising initiatives gradually lost momentum and impact.

"We'd spend months building something amazing," Michael explained, "then immediately shift our best people to the next big project. Within a year, our previous innovations were outdated, underutilized, or completely forgotten. We were working incredibly hard but not building sustainable value."

The breakthrough came when they shifted from organizing around projects to organizing around products - ongoing capabilities that required continuous investment, improvement, and evolution. Instead of forming temporary teams to complete specific initiatives, they created permanent teams responsible for the long-term success of particular product areas.

Their customer onboarding experience became a product owned by a dedicated team responsible for continuously improving conversion rates, reducing time-to-value, and enhancing user satisfaction. Their data analytics platform became a product with a team focused on expanding capabilities, improving performance, and anticipating customer needs. Their customer success function became a product area dedicated to increasing retention, identifying expansion opportunities, and gathering feedback for other product teams.

This shift required changes in how they measured success, allocated resources, and thought about career development. Instead of measuring project completion rates, they tracked product metrics: user engagement, business impact, competitive differentiation, and customer satisfaction. Instead of budget cycles tied to project phases, they implemented continuous funding models that allowed product teams to invest in improvements based on measured results and strategic priorities.

The results were transformative. Customer satisfaction scores increased by 40% because capabilities continued improving after launch rather than stagnating. Employee engagement improved because teams could see the long-term impact of their work. Innovation accelerated because product teams developed deep expertise in their domains and maintained close relationships with users.

Most importantly, StreamLine developed "compound capability" - the ability for improvements in one product area to enhance performance in others. Their onboarding improvements provided insights that enhanced their analytics platform. Their customer success learnings informed product development priorities. Their data capabilities enabled better onboarding personalization.

The shift from project to product thinking represents a fundamental change in how you view your organization's capabilities: not as a collection of completed initiatives but as a portfolio of living assets that require ongoing investment, continuous improvement, and strategic evolution.

Building Your Exponential Foundation

The companies that achieve sustainable exponential growth understand a truth that escapes most organizations: foundation isn't built once - it's cultivated continuously. Like the root system of a redwood forest, where individual trees are connected through an underground network that shares resources and information, your business foundation creates the invisible architecture that enables visible success.

Catherine and Karim from Teamworx didn't achieve their 340% growth advantage through a single breakthrough moment. They achieved it through systematic attention to the foundational elements that most companies treat as administrative overhead rather than strategic advantage. Their playbook became their competitive moat not because it contained secret insights but because it represented disciplined execution of fundamental principles that their competitors were too impatient to implement.

The eight elements we've explored - diverse strategy teams, North Star vision, ideal customer profiles, go-to-market alignment, agile organization structure, execution systems, high-performing teams, and product-centric thinking - work synergistically. Your North Star vision guides your customer selection, which informs your go-to-market strategy, which shapes your organizational structure, which enables your execution system, which attracts the right talent, which enables product-centric innovation.

When these elements align, something remarkable happens: your organization develops what resilience researchers call "antifragility" - the ability not just to survive disruption but to emerge stronger from challenges. You become the company that competitors study, customers recommend, and top talent seeks out.

The foundation you build today determines whether your organization will scale gracefully or struggle with the growing pains that destroy promising companies. The choice isn't whether to invest in foundation - it's whether to build it intentionally or allow it to emerge accidentally.

Your next ninety days will reveal whether you're serious about exponential growth or simply hoping for it. The companies that make the transition from hoping to achieving follow a specific sequence of foundation-building actions that create momentum and demonstrate commitment to systematic excellence.

Five Foundation-Building Actions for the Next Ninety Days

Conduct a Strategic Team Audit

Assess your current leadership team's cognitive diversity across four dimensions: thinking styles, professional backgrounds, personality types, and problem-solving approaches. Identify the most critical gap that's limiting your strategic decision-making quality. Either develop existing team members to fill this gap or begin recruiting someone whose strengths complement your team's current composition. Schedule weekly strategy sessions that require each team member to contribute their unique perspective on major decisions.

Crystallize Your Authentic North Star

Gather your top three customers, your five best employees, and your core leadership team for individual interviews about what your organization uniquely provides that wouldn't exist without you. Look for patterns in their responses that reveal your authentic value proposition. Craft a North Star statement that passes three tests: it's emotionally resonant (people feel something when they hear it), actionably specific (it guides decisions), and authentically unique (it couldn't describe another organization). Test this North Star by using it to evaluate three recent major decisions - does it provide clear guidance?

Define Your Ideal Customer Profile with Surgical Precision

Analyze your ten most successful customer relationships and identify the common characteristics that made these partnerships exceptional. Map the buying committee structure within these accounts and document the specific concerns, priorities, and decision-making criteria for each key persona. Create detailed profiles that go beyond demographics to include psychographics, behavioral patterns, and situational factors. Use these profiles to audit your current sales pipeline and identify which prospects are most likely to become ideal customers.

Implement a Quarterly OKR Cycle

Choose three company-level objectives that directly support your North Star vision and define two to three measurable key results for each objective. Cascade these objectives through your organization so every team and individual can articulate how their work contributes to company success. Establish a weekly rhythm for progress updates, monthly reviews for course corrections, and quarterly retrospectives for learning capture. Begin with a ninety-day pilot program to test the framework before full organizational implementation.

Transition One Initiative from Project to Product Mindset

Identify your most important recent "completed" project that could benefit from ongoing optimization and assign a permanent owner responsible for its long-term success. Define success metrics that extend beyond initial implementation to include user satisfaction, business impact, and continuous improvement. Allocate dedicated resources for ongoing enhancement rather than just maintenance. Create feedback loops with users to identify improvement opportunities and track how changes impact overall business performance. Use this pilot to demonstrate the value of product thinking before expanding the approach to other areas.

The foundation you build over the next ninety days will determine whether your organization joins the rare companies that achieve sustained exponential growth or remains among the majority that plateau after initial success. The choice - and the opportunity - is yours.

TEMPLATES

04

CHAPTER

The North Star, Vision and Mission

You're standing in front of your leadership team, asking a simple question that should have an immediate answer. "What drives us beyond profit?" The silence that follows isn't empty - it's deafening. Eyes dart around the conference room. Someone clears their throat. Another person reaches for their phone, suddenly remembering an urgent email.

This scenario played out in November 2023 in a meeting room in Berlin where I was consulting with a mid-market software company experiencing what their CEO called "success fatigue." Revenue was up 40% year-over-year, they'd just closed their Series C funding, yet something fundamental was broken. Employee turnover had spiked to 35%. Customer acquisition costs were climbing faster than revenue. Most telling of all, when we surveyed their 200-person workforce, we discovered something that should have sent shockwaves through every corner of that organization.

The results were eye-opening, though unfortunately not uncommon. More than 75% of all employees couldn't say what the company's vision was, and more than 50% of middle managers - the very people responsible for translating strategy into action - were unable to come up with anything resembling their company's vision. When we asked more questions, the root cause became crystal clear: employee engagement had flatlined, and a significant portion of their workforce felt no sense of meaning in their work beyond their bi-weekly paycheck.

Here's what makes this particularly troubling for leaders like you. They had spent considerable time and resources developing what they believed was a compelling mission statement. It was prominently displayed on their website, printed on elegant plaques in the lobby, and referenced in quarterly all-hands meetings. The problem wasn't that they lacked a mission statement - the problem was that it had become corporate wallpaper, invisible and irrelevant to the people who mattered most.

Let me be clear about something that might challenge conventional wisdom: a North Star Vision is not the typical mission or vision statement that you'd find on a company website. Those polished paragraphs crafted by marketing committees and wordsmithed to perfection? They're often beautifully written and completely meaningless for the people who actually do the work. They sound impressive in board presentations and look professional on annual reports, but they fail the most critical test of all - they don't inspire anyone to get out of bed on Monday morning with purpose.

A North Star vision is also not a revenue target or profit goal. It's not about hitting $100 million ARR or achieving 25% EBITDA margins, though those outcomes may naturally follow. When leaders confuse financial metrics with vision, they essentially ask their teams to care about shareholder returns as much as they do. Here's the uncomfortable truth: most employees don't lie awake at night worried about quarterly earnings per share, and they shouldn't have to.

What we're talking about instead is something far more powerful and fundamentally different. A North Star vision represents the magnetic force that pulls every initiative, every decision, and every individual contribution toward a common destination that transcends the boundaries of traditional business objectives. It answers the question that every human being asks, whether consciously or subconsciously, when they invest their life energy in an organization: "Why does this work matter beyond the money I earn?"

This distinction isn't academic - it's practical and measurable. Organizations that successfully implement authentic North Star visions create what researchers call "purpose-driven engagement," which translates into tangible business outcomes that traditional mission statements simply cannot deliver. We're talking about reduced turnover, increased innovation rates, improved customer satisfaction scores, and yes, stronger financial performance. But these results emerge as natural byproducts of something deeper: a workforce that understands exactly how their daily contributions connect to something meaningful.

The challenge for technology leaders like yourself lies in recognizing that the very analytical skills that make you successful in optimizing systems, debugging code, and scaling operations can sometimes work against you when it comes to creating emotional connection and meaning. You're comfortable with metrics, algorithms, and logical frameworks - and those tools remain valuable. But developing a North Star vision requires you to engage with the messier, more human aspects of leadership that can't be reduced to spreadsheets or flowcharts.

Consider the fundamental shift happening in today's workforce, particularly among the talented professionals you need to attract and retain. The traditional employment contract - we pay you well, you work hard, everyone goes home happy - has evolved into something more sophisticated. Today's knowledge workers, especially those in technology, are asking deeper questions about purpose, impact, and legacy. They want to know that their expertise is contributing to something worthwhile, not just something profitable.

Beyond Corporate Poetry: Defining Your True North

What happens when a company discovers its authentic reason for existing? I witnessed this transformation firsthand while working with a rapidly scaling fintech startup that was struggling to maintain its culture through explosive growth. The breakthrough came during what seemed like an ordinary brainstorming session, but the results were anything but ordinary.

One of their board members, Sarah, shared something personal that changed everything. She revealed her deep commitment to education in underserved communities and proposed the company dedicate a portion of their profits to funding educational initiatives in developing countries. What started as one person's passion quickly ignited something powerful across the entire leadership team. They weren't just discussing corporate social responsibility - they were uncovering their collective soul.

Within that same month, this fintech company made a decision that redefined their identity. They committed 25% of their profits to a fund supporting educational access for children in underserved regions of Africa. But here's where the magic happened: they didn't just write a check and call it philanthropy. They fundamentally restructured how they measured and communicated success.

Instead of celebrating quarterly revenue milestones in their all-hands meetings, they started reporting "students funded" and "schools built." Every internal presentation that previously showcased dollar amounts was translated into these new metrics. Conference room displays featured photos of the schools they'd helped construct and stories of individual students whose lives had been changed. The company's Slack channels buzzed with updates from their education partners, creating an emotional connection between lines of code written in Berlin and Warsaw and children learning to read in rural Kenya.

The transformation was measurable and immediate. When we conducted follow-up interviews with employees six months later, 100% of those surveyed could articulate the company's vision with clarity and passion. More importantly, they reported feeling fully committed to exceeding every task they'd been given, not because of performance bonuses or stock options, but because they understood the direct connection between their work and educational opportunities for children who might otherwise never set foot in a classroom.

This illustrates the essence of a North Star vision: it's the one guiding statement that unites all initiatives of an organization behind something larger than itself. But notice what makes this different from typical corporate mission statements. It's not abstract or aspirational - it's concrete and actionable. It's not something that requires interpretation - it's immediately understandable. Most critically, it's not something that employees have to be convinced to care about - it's something they naturally want to be part of.

The power of an authentic North Star vision lies in its ability to transform individual job descriptions into collective mission participation. When your software engineers understand that the authentication system they're building will protect the financial data that enables educational funding, their work takes on new meaning. When your sales team knows every contract they close translates directly into learning opportunities for children, their conversations with prospects become more purposeful and passionate.

Yanik Silver captured this beautifully in his book *Evolved Enterprise* when he highlighted the philosophy of Greyston Bakery. Their mission statement breaks every conventional rule about corporate messaging:

"We don't hire people to bake brownies; we bake brownies to hire people." This isn't marketing copy - it's a fundamental redefinition of business purpose that inverts traditional thinking about profit and purpose.

Greyston's North Star vision demonstrates how powerful simplicity can be. Every employee, from entry-level bakers to senior management, can immediately understand how their role serves the larger mission. There's no ambiguity about priorities, no confusion about what success looks like, and no need for extensive explanation about why the work matters. The vision is simultaneously their business model, their hiring philosophy, and their competitive advantage.

A North Star vision should be shaped in a way employees and customers can relate to, carries genuine meaning for the people who interact with it, and creates unity rather than division. It becomes the filter through which every decision gets made, the inspiration that drives innovation, and the standard against which performance gets measured.

The Coherence Imperative: Why Alignment Isn't Optional

Three weeks ago, I received a frustrated call from Klaus, CTO of a promising startup that had just secured a big round of funding. Despite their technical achievements and market traction, something was fundamentally broken. "Jürgen," he said, "we're building incredible technology, but it feels like we're running in circles. Everyone's working hard, but nobody seems to be working toward the same thing."

This scenario reveals one of the most overlooked challenges in scaling technology organizations: the coherence crisis. As companies grow beyond the startup phase where everyone naturally knows everyone else's role, maintaining alignment becomes exponentially more complex. Without a unifying North Star vision, even the most talented teams begin operating in silos, pursuing objectives that may be individually logical but collectively counterproductive.

Here's the litmus test that every leader should apply: if anyone in your organization can't come to work every day and articulate how their specific work connects to your company's North Star vision, one of three critical failures has occurred. Either there is no authentic vision driving the organization, there's a massive middle management problem preventing the connection between daily work and overarching purpose, or people are working on initiatives that fundamentally don't align with where the company should be heading.

This isn't only about employee satisfaction or corporate culture - though those matter enormously. This is about operational efficiency and competitive advantage in markets where the difference between thriving and surviving often comes down to how quickly and effectively organizations can mobilize their collective intelligence toward shared objectives.

Research conducted by Deloitte across more than 3,000 companies over a five-year period reveals something that should capture the attention of every performance-focused leader: companies with a North Star vision that every employee can relate to and that meaningfully connects individual work to universal purpose are 78% more successful than their competitors across multiple metrics including revenue growth, employee retention, customer satisfaction, and market share expansion.

But what does "78% more successful" mean in practical terms? Let's break this down into metrics that matter to technology leaders. These organizations experience 31% lower employee turnover, which in today's competitive talent market translates to significant savings in recruitment, onboarding, and productivity ramp-up costs. They achieve 67% higher employee engagement scores, which correlates directly with innovation rates and quality of output. Perhaps most importantly, they demonstrate 42% faster decision-making processes because alignment around shared vision eliminates much of the debate and analysis paralysis that plague organizations lacking clear direction.

The mechanism behind these improvements isn't mysterious - it's psychological and practical. When people understand how their individual contributions connect to something meaningful, several powerful dynamics emerge simultaneously. First, they become more willing to take ownership of problems and solutions beyond their immediate job descriptions. Second, they naturally prioritize activities that advance the shared mission over tasks that merely fulfill their personal performance metrics. Third, they develop what organizational psychologists call "mission-driven creativity," generating innovations that serve the larger purpose rather than just optimizing local processes.

Reflect on what happened at Patagonia under the leadership of Yvon Chouinard. Their North Star vision of environmental stewardship didn't just influence their marketing or corporate social responsibility initiatives - it fundamentally shaped product development, supply chain decisions, hiring practices, and even their approach to customer service. When everyone from fabric designers to customer service representatives understands that their work directly contributes to environmental protection, decision-making becomes faster, more consistent, and more innovative.

Bringing coherence to the work of everyone in your organization isn't just a nice-to-have leadership aspiration - it's the foundational requirement for sustained high performance in complex, rapidly changing markets. This is what a well-crafted North Star vision delivers: it transforms individual job descriptions into collective mission participation, creating the kind of organizational alignment that competitors struggle to replicate.

The Collaborative Compass: Building Vision Through Collective Wisdom

Last year, I facilitated a North Star vision development process for a business process optimization software company that had grown from 25 to 300 employees in just eighteen months. Their CEO, Julien, initially wanted to lock himself in a conference room for a weekend and emerge with their company's defining vision statement. "I know this business better than anyone," he argued. "Shouldn't the vision come from the top?"

This impulse is understandable but fundamentally flawed. Creating authentic North Star statements requires a collaborative process that typically unfolds over four to six intensive working sessions with a diverse group of senior stakeholders forming what we call a vision group. The magic happens not in isolation but in the dynamic tension of different perspectives colliding, challenging assumptions, and ultimately synthesizing into something none of them could have created individually.

The composition of your vision group matters enormously. You want voices from different functions - engineering, sales, marketing, customer success, operations - but also different thinking styles and organizational tenures. Include the skeptic who asks hard questions, the visionary who sees possibilities others miss, the pragmatist who grounds ideas in reality, and the connector who understands how different stakeholders will respond. Typically, six to eight people create the right balance between diverse input and productive dialogue.

Consider bringing in an objective facilitator who can guide and structure these sessions without influencing the final content. A skilled moderator serves multiple critical functions: ensuring that all group members remain fully engaged rather than deferring to the highest-ranking person in the room, questioning assumptions that might otherwise go unchallenged, managing conflict when passionate disagreement threatens to derail progress, and focusing creative efforts toward the desired outcome without constraining the organic emergence of ideas.

Here's what many leaders miss: you don't need to start from a blank page, staring at an empty whiteboard hoping for inspiration to strike. Begin by clarifying the fundamental definitions that often get confused in organizational discussions. What's the difference between purpose, mission, vision, and values statements? How do they complement rather than compete with each other? Make sure your vision group understands not only their individual functions but how they work together to create organizational coherence.

Encourage team members to research and reflect on North Star statements from other organizations - within your industry and from companies that inspire them personally. Ask them to analyze what makes certain statements memorable and motivating while others feel generic and forgettable. What language choices create emotional connection? Which examples demonstrate clear linkage between vision and operational decisions? How do the most effective statements balance aspiration with achievability?

While there's no absolute correct sequence for developing these statements, experience suggests starting with core values often proves most productive. Values are generally more accessible for people to identify and articulate because everyone is either already experiencing them in the organization's day-to-day culture or acutely aware of their absence. Beginning with something concrete gets the creative conversation flowing and builds confidence in the group's ability to tackle more abstract concepts.

Core values reflect the behaviors and principles that guide your organization's operations in practice, not just in theory. They shape daily interactions, establish standards for decision-making, and create the cultural foundation upon which everything else gets built. Think of them as the behavioral DNA that determines how your organization responds to opportunities, challenges, and unexpected situations.

Here's a practical approach that consistently produces meaningful results: have your vision team generate an initial list of existing values they observe in the organization and aspirational values they believe should guide future growth. Simultaneously, survey the broader organization asking people to select words that characterize the values currently shaping your culture and suggest new values that should be considered. This dual approach builds buy-in through participation while providing the vision team with broader organizational input to consider.

The key is narrowing your values to approximately four to six core principles. More than this creates diminishing returns and makes it difficult for people to remember and prioritize what matters most. It's perfectly acceptable - even beneficial - to include one or two aspirational values that represent growth areas for your organization. However, if all your values are aspirational or contrary to people's daily lived experiences, you risk generating cynicism or outright rejection when you attempt to implement them.

Your Navigation Blueprint: Five Steps to North Star Clarity

The journey from corporate mission statement to authentic North Star vision doesn't happen overnight, but it doesn't require years of strategic planning either. What it demands is intentional focus, collaborative commitment, and systematic execution. After guiding dozens of technology leaders through this transformation, I've distilled the process into five actionable steps that consistently produce meaningful results.

These aren't theoretical frameworks or abstract concepts - they're practical tools that you can implement immediately, whether you're leading a fifty-person startup or a 5,000-person enterprise. Each step builds upon the previous one, creating momentum that carries your organization toward the clarity and alignment that high-performing teams require.

The beauty of this approach lies in its adaptability. You might discover that your organization already has some elements in place, allowing you to accelerate certain phases. Alternatively, you might find that particular steps require additional time and attention based on your unique circumstances. The key is maintaining forward progress while remaining responsive to what emerges during the process.

Remember, developing a North Star vision isn't about finding the perfect words - it's about creating authentic connection between individual purpose and collective mission. The most powerful visions aren't necessarily the most eloquent; they're the ones that generate genuine enthusiasm and sustained commitment from the people who matter most to your organization's success. If your North Star doesn't resonate with your employees and customers it should be changed.

STEP 1

Assemble Your Vision Architects

Form a diverse vision group of six to eight senior leaders representing different functions, thinking styles, & organizational perspectives. Include longtime employees who understand your cultural foundation and newer team members who bring fresh viewpoints. Schedule four to six working sessions of ninety minutes each, spaced one week apart, to allow reflection between meetings. Secure executive sponsorship and ensure all participants can commit to the full process - partial engagement produces partial results.

STEP 2

Uncover Your Value Foundation

Begin with values discovery rather than vision crafting. Survey your entire organization, asking people to identify existing values they observe daily and aspirational values they believe should guide future decisions. Have your vision group analyze these responses alongside their own observations to identify for to six core principles that authentically reflect current reality and desired evolution. Test these values against recent organizational decisions to ensure they're genuine rather than aspirational corporate poetry.

STEP 3

Design Your Magnetic Statement

Develop your North Star vision statement using these criteria: it must be immediately understandable by every employee, emotionally compelling enough to inspire voluntary extra effort, specific enough to guide decision-making, and connected to something larger than financial performance. Employees should feel pride about being part of this vision. Study examples from organizations you admire, but resist copying their language. Your North Star must emerge from your unique combination of values, capabilities, and aspirations.

STEP 4

Test and Refine Through Reality

Before announcing your North Star vision, test it with trusted employees outside the vision group through informal conversations and small focus groups. Ask them: "Does this reflect why you're proud to work here? Can you see how your role contributes to this larger purpose? Would this statement help you prioritize competing demands?" Use their feedback to refine language, clarify meaning, and strengthen emotional connection. This step prevents the all-too-common scenario of leadership teams falling in love with statements that leave employees cold.

STEP 5

Integrate into Organizational DNA

Launch your North Star vision through storytelling rather than presentation slides. Share the journey of how it was developed, the insights that shaped it, and specific examples of how it will influence daily decisions. Create measurement systems that track progress toward vision-related outcomes alongside financial metrics. Most importantly, model the behavior yourself - reference the North Star vision in your own decision-making, celebrate examples of employees living these values, and consistently demonstrate that this isn't just another corporate initiative but a fundamental shift in how your organization operates.

The path from wherever you are today to authentic North Star clarity isn't always linear, but it's always worthwhile. When your people understand not only what they're building but why it matters beyond profit margins, you unlock the kind of organizational energy that transforms good companies into exceptional ones. The question isn't whether you can afford to invest in this process - it's whether you can afford not to.

05

CHAPTER

Who Is Your Ideal Customer?

The Mirror Moment: When Assumptions Shatter Reality

The conference room in Paris fell silent. Ten weeks of intensive customer interviews had culminated in this moment, and what we'd discovered would fundamentally reshape everything this SaaS company thought they knew about their business.

Sarah, the VP of Marketing, stared at the data sprawled across the whiteboard. "You're telling me that everything we believed about our customers was wrong?"

Not wrong, I explained, but dangerously incomplete. Like most organizations, they had built their entire go-to-market strategy on a foundation of assumptions - educated guesses masquerading as customer insights. The numbers looked impressive on their dashboards: conversion rates, lifetime value, churn metrics. But beneath these statistics lay a gap between what they thought their customers wanted and what actually drove purchasing decisions.

This is quite common. In my experience helping software and IT companies accelerate growth, I'm consistently surprised by how little most organizations truly know about their key customers. They can tell you demographic data, usage patterns, and revenue figures, but ask them why customers really buy, who influences the decision, or what personal goals drive their champions and you'll often encounter blank stares.

The company in question - let's call them DataFlow Solutions - was experiencing the classic symptoms of customer blindness. Revenue had plateaued despite increasing marketing spend. Sales cycles were getting longer. Deals were stalling in the pipeline with mysterious "we need more time to evaluate" responses. Sound familiar?

When we began our deep-dive investigation, DataFlow's customer profile looked clean and logical on paper. Their "ideal customer" was defined as mid-market software companies with fifty to 200 employees, annual revenue between $10 to 50 million, and a need for data integration solutions. Simple, measurable, and completely inadequate for driving real growth.

The problem wasn't their data - it was their depth. And data can only lead to assumptions that need to be verified by interviewing real people. They knew the what but had never explored the why, the who, and the how that truly determine whether a prospect becomes a customer, and more importantly, whether that customer becomes an advocate who drives exponential growth.

Theodore Levitt's famous insight rings particularly true in our data-driven age: "People don't want to buy a quarter-inch drill. They want a quarter-inch hole." Yet most companies remain fixated on their drill specifications while completely missing the holes their customers are desperately trying to create.

Here's what shifted everything for DataFlow Solutions: we stopped talking about features and started understanding outcomes. We moved beyond demographics to psychographics. We stopped focusing solely on decision-makers and began mapping entire buying committees. Most crucially, we started asking not just what our customers bought, but why they bought it, how it helped them personally, and what would happen if they didn't solve their challenge.

The transformation was remarkable. Within twelve months, their sales grew by 22%, and their pipeline expanded by 47%. But perhaps more importantly, they evolved from a vendor competing on features to a strategic partner solving meaningful business problems.

Your customers aren't statistics in a CRM system. They're human beings with careers to advance, problems to solve, and personal reputations on the line. They're navigating complex organizational dynamics, managing multiple stakeholders, and balancing competing priorities. Understanding these layers of complexity isn't just nice to have - it's the difference between sustainable growth and endless frustration.

The companies that thrive in today's competitive landscape share one crucial characteristic: they know their ideal customers so intimately that every message resonates, every solution addresses real pain, and every interaction builds deeper trust. They've moved beyond the surface-level attributes that anyone can identify to the profound insights that only come from genuine curiosity and systematic investigation.

This chapter will equip you with the framework to achieve that level of customer intimacy. You'll learn how to identify your true ideal customers, map the complex web of stakeholders who influence purchasing decisions, and create value propositions so compelling that prospects feel, as Alex Hormozi puts it, "stupid saying no."

But first, we need to shatter some comfortable myths about who your customers really are.

Beyond Demographics: Discovering Your Value Catalyst

To better illustrate, take the following scenario: you're reviewing your CRM data, and two companies appear nearly identical. Both are $25 million software firms with 120 employees, located in major metropolitan areas, using similar technology stacks. Your traditional customer profiling would classify them as equally valuable prospects. Yet one becomes a loyal advocate who refers millions in new business, while the other churns after six months, citing "lack of ROI."

What made the difference? The answer lies in a fundamental shift in how we define ideal customers.

Your ideal customer isn't the customer you wish you had - it's the customer you can provide the highest value to with your products or services. This distinction transforms everything about how you approach market identification, sales conversations, and customer success initiatives.

During our DataFlow Solutions investigation, this principle revealed itself dramatically. Their highest-spending customers weren't necessarily their most profitable or satisfied ones. In fact, some large enterprises were draining resources through excessive support requests and custom development demands, while smaller companies with specific integration challenges were becoming passionate advocates.

The breakthrough came when we started asking different questions. Instead of "Who spends the most?" we asked "Who achieves the most dramatic outcomes?" Rather than "What's their company size?" we explored "What's their transformation story?"

Think about how your prospect gains value from using your product or service. Can you articulate, with mathematical precision, the business impact you create? Most companies struggle here because they've never quantified their value from the customer's perspective. They know their features but not their outcomes. They understand their process but not their customer's journey. The only way to truly understand the impact of your solutions is by having conversations with your customers. Data alone will never give you the complete picture.

As an example, the financial services company that implemented our client's analytics platform. The obvious value was "better data insights." The real value was enabling their chief risk officer to identify fraud patterns seventy-two hours faster, preventing an average of $2.3 million in losses monthly. That specificity transforms a generic software sale into a career-defining partnership.

Understanding how your customers make money - and how your offering amplifies their success - creates the foundation for everything that follows. DataFlow discovered that their most successful customers weren't just buying data integration; they were buying competitive advantage through faster time-to-market for new products.

Customer value extends beyond financial metrics. You need to understand the market forces shaping your customer's industry. What trends are driving urgency? What regulations are creating compliance pressure? What competitive dynamics are forcing innovation? To truly understand these aspects, you need to talk to real people. Don't just trust assumptions and data, verify them by talking to customers and prospects.

One software development firm we worked with found their ideal customers weren't just companies needing custom applications - they were businesses facing digital transformation deadlines imposed by changing customer expectations. The external pressure created urgency that made price objections disappear and decision cycles accelerate.

Who are your customer's competitors, and how does that competitive landscape influence their strategic priorities? A marketing automation company discovered that their most valuable customers were firms losing market share to digitally-native competitors. This insight allowed them to position their solution not as a marketing tool but as a competitive recovery system.

The strategy question becomes crucial: What are your customer's core initiatives for achieving their goals? How does your solution become integral to their success rather than peripheral to their operations?

During customer interviews, we learned that DataFlow's champions weren't just trying to integrate data - they were attempting to prove the value of their entire data science teams to skeptical executives. Our solution became their proof point, their career advancement tool, their internal credibility builder.

This level of understanding transforms your sales conversations. Instead of explaining features, you're discussing business transformation. Rather than competing on price, you're partnering on outcomes. Instead of selling to budgets, you're creating investment cases that generate their own budgets.

The most successful organizations we've worked with can articulate their customer's success metrics better than many customers can themselves. They understand the domino effect their solution creates:

how solving one problem enables three others, how efficiency gains in one department create capacity for strategic initiatives elsewhere.

When you truly understand who can receive maximum value from your offering, everything else becomes clearer: your messaging, your pricing, your product development roadmap, even your hiring priorities. You stop trying to be everything to everyone and start becoming indispensable to someone.

The Hidden Orchestra: Mapping Your Customer's Buying Symphony

What if I told you that the person who signed your last major contract wasn't actually the one who decided to buy from you?

This insight struck me during a post-mortem interview with DataFlow's largest enterprise client. The CEO had signed the million-dollar agreement, but the real decision architect was Maria, a senior data analyst whose frustration with manual reporting processes had sparked a six-month internal campaign for change. She had built the business case, influenced the IT director, convinced the CFO, and essentially orchestrated the entire purchasing decision from behind the scenes.

Most B2B sales failures happen because companies focus on the visible decision-maker while ignoring the invisible influencers. It's like trying to conduct an orchestra while only watching the first violin, missing the intricate interplay of instruments that creates the full symphony.

Understanding the buying committee isn't academic exercise - it's survival strategy. In today's complex B2B environment, the average purchasing decision involves 7 stakeholders, each with distinct motivations, concerns, and success criteria. Miss even one key player and your perfect solution can die in committee review.

The buying committee consists of four distinct roles, each wielding different types of influence over your deal's outcome.

- **Champions**

  Champions are your internal advocates, typically end-users or department heads who will directly benefit from your solution. They're the ones attending discovery calls, preparing comparison reports, and translating your value proposition into language their organization understands. In smaller companies, the champion and decision-maker might be the same person - often the CEO personally invested in solving specific operational challenges.

  During our DataFlow research, champions were consistently data scientists and analysts frustrated by spending 60% of their time on data preparation instead of analysis. They weren't just buying integration software; they were buying career satisfaction and professional growth opportunities.

- **Decision-makers**

  Decision-makers hold budget authority and contract-signing power. While they rarely participate in detailed product evaluations, they rely heavily on champion recommendations and business case presentations. In mid-market and enterprise organizations, decision-makers typically delegate research to champions while focusing on strategic implications and ROI justification.

The critical insight here is understanding what decision-makers need to feel confident in their approval. It's rarely about technical specifications - it's about risk mitigation, competitive advantage, and organizational reputation.

- **Influencers**

Influencers don't directly participate in vendor evaluation, but their opinions can make or break deals. They might be consulted during team meetings, asked for informal advice, or their past experiences might be referenced in decision discussions. External consultants, board members, or respected internal leaders often play influencer roles.

One DataFlow deal nearly collapsed when an influential board member questioned the wisdom of "another software purchase" during a strategic planning session. We saved the deal by providing the CEO with talking points that reframed our solution as infrastructure investment rather than software expense.

- **Blockers**

Blockers represent the most dangerous category because they're often invisible until it's too late. These stakeholders see your solution as threatening their interests, questioning their expertise, or competing with their preferred approaches. They might worry about job security, departmental relevance, or simply resist change on principle.

Identifying potential blockers requires sophisticated investigation. Who might feel threatened by process changes your solution enables? Which departments could lose influence or resources? Who has advocated for competing approaches in the past?

The DataFlow team learned this lesson painfully when a major deal stalled indefinitely. Post-investigation revealed that the IT security director - never mentioned in previous conversations - had concerns about data access protocols. Rather than voicing objections directly, he delayed approval processes until the budget cycle expired.

Understanding personas within buying committees goes beyond job titles to encompass professional goals, personal motivations, and individual risk tolerance. What KPIs drive each stakeholder's performance reviews? What career advancement goals shape their decision criteria? What personal fears or aspirations influence their evaluation process?

A champion might support your solution because it could eliminate weekend work and improve work-life balance. A decision-maker might approve it because successful implementation enhances their reputation as an innovative leader. An influencer might endorse it because they've seen similar solutions succeed elsewhere.

But personas aren't just about individual psychology - they're about organizational dynamics. How do different departments interact? What historical tensions exist between teams? Which stakeholders have collaborated successfully before, and which relationships require careful navigation?

The most revealing insight from our DataFlow investigation was discovering that their most successful deals happened when IT directors and business users had previous positive collaboration experiences. Companies with adversarial IT-business relationships consistently struggled with implementation, regardless of technical fit.

This understanding transforms your approach from selling to individuals to orchestrating organizational alignment. You begin designing touchpoints that bring stakeholders together, creating shared ownership of outcomes rather than departmental competition over resources.

And never forget the CFO. I remember having an eye-opening conversation with a CFO. I asked him how he evaluates purchasing decisions. He stated: "I am approaching investment decisions with a default "no". Every proposal comes with a great ROI and if all of them where true our company would be a bank. If I don't understand why our company would need to invest in a solution and how this solution will support us in achieving our goals I will not approve. I also need to understand what the risks are and what the risk mitigation strategy is."

I then asked him how to best reach out to CFOs. He stated:" As a CFO I don't want to talk to vendors and most of the CFOs I know don't want to talk to vendors as well." He recommended preparing a concise proposal starting with the "why" followed by the how, the risks and the risk mitigation strategy.

The Pain Equation: Solving What Really Matters

"If you really understood what this reporting process was doing to my weekends, you'd realize why I'm willing to fight for this budget."

Those words, spoken by a frustrated analytics director during one of our DataFlow interviews, revealed something profound about the nature of business pain. It's not just about operational inefficiencies or budget constraints - it's deeply personal.

The most successful salespeople I know have mastered the pain equation: corporate pain + personal pain = buying urgency. Miss either side of this equation and your deal lacks the emotional fuel necessary to overcome organizational inertia.

Corporate pain is relatively straightforward to identify. These are the business challenges keeping executives awake at night: declining market share, regulatory compliance requirements, competitive threats, or operational inefficiencies. They're measurable, reportable, and often discussed openly in business strategy sessions.

But personal pain? That's where the real motivation lies, and it's rarely discussed in boardrooms.

Take the example of DataFlow's analytics director who became our strongest champion. His corporate pain was clear: manual data integration was consuming forty hours weekly of his team's time, delaying critical business reports. But his personal pain ran deeper. Those delays were making him look incompetent to senior leadership. He was missing his daughter's soccer games to meet reporting deadlines. His team was burning out and considering other opportunities.

The solution wasn't only improving operational efficiency - it was securing his professional reputation and restoring his work-life balance.

Understanding this dual nature of pain changes everything about how you position your offering. You're not just solving business problems; you're addressing human struggles. You're not just improving processes; you're changing lives.

Think about how your offering helps personas within your ideal customer achieve their professional goals more effectively. Does it accelerate their path to promotion? Does it enhance their visibility within the organization? Does it free up time for strategic initiatives that showcase their leadership capabilities?

A marketing automation platform doesn't merely generate leads - it makes marketing directors look brilliant to their CEOs. A cybersecurity solution doesn't just prevent breaches - it helps IT leaders sleep soundly knowing their careers won't be destroyed by a single successful attack.

The personal dimension extends beyond career advancement to encompass psychological comfort. What fears does your solution alleviate? What anxieties does it eliminate? What confidence does it restore?

During our research, we discovered that DataFlow's champions shared a common psychological profile: they all struggled with imposter syndrome. Despite their expertise, manual processes made them feel technically incompetent compared to colleagues at more advanced organizations. Our solution didn't only automate workflows - it restored professional confidence.

This insight transformed their messaging. Instead of emphasizing technical capabilities, they highlighted how their platform helped data professionals achieve their full potential. Sales conversations shifted from feature demonstrations to career development discussions.

But pain isn't always obvious, and the most significant opportunities often involve pain that prospects haven't yet recognized or articulated.

Sometimes your role is educational - helping customers understand problems they didn't know they had.

One of DataFlow's most successful expansions happened when they helped a customer realize their "acceptable" reporting delays cost them competitive advantages. The client normalized four-day turnaround times for market analysis, not recognizing competitors with real-time insights were consistently out-maneuvering them in client presentations.

The key is asking better questions during customer interactions. Instead of "What challenges are you facing?" try "What would become possible if this problem disappeared?" Rather than "How does this impact your operations?" explore "How does this affect your team's morale and confidence?"

Pain intensity varies dramatically across stakeholders. What feels like a minor inconvenience to a decision-maker might represent a career-threatening crisis to a champion. Understanding these different pain thresholds helps you calibrate your messaging for maximum impact with each audience.

The CFO might view manual reporting as a minor efficiency issue worth $50,000 annually. The analytics manager sees it as a professional competency crisis worth whatever it takes to solve. Speak to the CFO about ROI; speak to the manager about career advancement and team satisfaction.

Pain evolves throughout the buying cycle. Initial pain might focus on immediate operational challenges, but as implementation approaches, new concerns emerge: change management anxiety, training requirements, integration complexity. Anticipating this evolution allows you to address concerns before they become objections.

The Total Cost Reality: Beyond Price Tags and Contracts

Here's a question that will revolutionize how you think about pricing: What if the biggest cost your customers face isn't your subscription fee but the three months of executive meetings required to evaluate your solution and the time internal teams need to spend during planning, implementation and onboarding?

Most companies catastrophically underestimate the true investment their prospects make during the buying and implementation process. They obsess over subscription prices and implementation fees while completely ignoring the hidden costs that are often higher than their actual charges.

The Total Cost Reality encompasses five distinct investment categories that prospects evaluate, often subconsciously, when deciding whether to move forward with your solution.

Time Investment

Time investment represents the most significant hidden cost in B2B purchasing. Keep in mind the executive hours consumed during your typical sales cycle: initial research, vendor meetings, internal discussions, proposal reviews, reference calls, and contract negotiations. At DataFlow, we calculated that their average enterprise deal required 120 hours of customer time across multiple stakeholders. For senior executives earning $200-plus per hour, that's $24,000 in opportunity cost before anyone signs a contract.

This time investment extends beyond the sales process into implementation & adoption phases. Training sessions, data migration, workflow adjustments, & change management initiatives can consume hundreds of additional hours across the organization. Smart buyers factor this reality into their decision-making, even if they don't articulate it explicitly.

An often forgotten aspect is that you are not only competing on budget but also on internal resources. If internal resource is blocked for your project, it can't be used for other initiatives.

The most successful companies I work with minimize time investment through streamlined evaluation processes, comprehensive self-service resources, and implementation methodologies that reduce customer resource requirements. They understand that reducing friction accelerates decisions more effectively than reducing prices.

Risk Investment

Risk investment might be the most psychologically powerful factor influencing purchase decisions. Every new solution introduces potential failure points: implementation delays, adoption challenges, integration complications, or performance disappointments. For individual stakeholders, these risks aren't just operational - they're career-threatening.

The DataFlow team learned this lesson when a major prospect's evaluation stalled for six months. The IT director privately confided that a previous software implementation had failed spectacularly, resulting in public criticism and damaged credibility. He wasn't just evaluating technical capabilities - he was protecting his professional reputation.

Understanding risk perception allows you to design de-risking strategies that accelerate decisions. Pilot programs, phased implementations, success guarantees, and comprehensive support commitments can dramatically reduce perceived risk without affecting your pricing structure.

Reputation Investment

Reputation investment affects every stakeholder involved in the purchasing decision. Champions stake their credibility on vendor selection. Decision-makers link their leadership reputation to project outcomes. Even influencers risk social capital when endorsing solutions to colleagues. In case you are competing with a dominant market leader, decision makers also need to defend their decision for your solution.

During customer interviews, we discovered that DataFlow's most successful deals happened when champions could point to peer organizations with similar challenges who had achieved remarkable results. Social proof wasn't mere nice-to-have marketing material - it was essential risk mitigation for career-conscious professionals.

Opportunity Cost Investment

Opportunity cost investment represents the most sophisticated aspect of total cost reality. Which other strategic initiatives get delayed while resources focus on vendor evaluation and implementation? What competitive advantages are missed during transition periods? What growth opportunities remain unexplored while teams adapt to new workflows?

A manufacturing client once told me they postponed a major product launch because their analytics team was consumed with software implementation. The delayed launch cost them six months of market opportunity - a far greater investment than any software subscription.

Political Capital Investment

Political capital investment reflects the internal negotiations required to secure budget approval, gain stakeholder buy-in, and navigate organizational dynamics. Every purchase decision consumes relationship capital within the organization. Champions must cash in favors to secure support. Decision-makers must balance competing departmental priorities.

This political dimension explains why some technically superior solutions lose to inferior alternatives with stronger internal advocates. The "best" solution isn't always the one with the most features - it's the one requiring the least political capital to approve.

Understanding total cost reality transforms your value proposition from feature-benefit presentations to investment-return conversations. Instead of justifying your price, you optimize their investment across all five categories.

The perceived value of your offering must exceed the total investment across time, risk, reputation, opportunity cost, and political capital. This multi-dimensional value equation explains why price objections often mask deeper concerns about these hidden costs.

Smart positioning addresses each investment category explicitly. Demonstrate how your solution minimizes time requirements through automated onboarding. Showcase risk mitigation through proven implementation methodologies. Provide reputation insurance through comprehensive success stories. Address opportunity costs by highlighting accelerated time-to-value.

The companies that master total cost reality don't compete on price - they compete on investment efficiency. They don't simply sell solutions; they optimize their customers' entire decision-making and implementation experience.

The Irresistible Proposition: Crafting Offers They Can't Refuse

The moment you shift from selling features to selling transformations, everything changes. Your conversations evolve from vendor pitches to strategic consultations. Your pricing discussions transform from cost justification to investment optimization. Most importantly, your close rates accelerate because prospects stop evaluating whether they can afford your solution and start calculating whether they can afford to delay it.

The challenge isn't just making your offer attractive - it's making it irresistible to people who evaluate success differently, face distinct risks, and measure ROI through entirely different lenses.

During the DataFlow transformation, we discovered their original value proposition focused almost exclusively on technical capabilities. "Advanced data integration with real-time processing and enterprise-grade security." Impressive features but completely divorced from the outcomes that motivated buying decisions.

The breakthrough came when we reverse-engineered their most successful deals to understand what made customers say yes immediately versus what triggered months of evaluation paralysis.

Value Perception Varies by Persona

Your champion evaluates your offer through the lens of daily operational impact. They want to know: Will this make my job easier? Will this enhance my professional reputation? Will this free me from weekend work and late-night emergency calls?

For DataFlow's analytics champions, the irresistible value wasn't faster processing speeds - it was the ability to deliver insights proactively instead of reactively. Instead of spending weekends troubleshooting data issues, they could spend Monday morning presenting strategic recommendations to executive teams.

Decision-makers evaluate offers through strategic business impact. They need to understand: How does this advance our competitive position? What organizational capabilities does this enable? How does this align with our long-term strategic objectives?

The same DataFlow solution that gave champions work-life balance gave CEOs competitive intelligence capabilities that influenced market timing decisions worth millions in revenue impact.

Influencers and blockers evaluate offers through change management implications. They want to know: How will this affect existing relationships and power dynamics? What new requirements will this create for their teams? How does this compare to alternative approaches they've advocated?

The Multi-Dimensional Value Framework

Creating irresistible offers requires simultaneously addressing four value dimensions: functional, emotional, social, and economic.

FUNCTIONAL VALUE

Functional value addresses the practical problem-solving capabilities of your solution. This is where most companies focus their positioning and where most differentiation attempts fail because competitors can easily replicate functional benefits.

EMOTIONAL VALUE

Emotional value addresses the psychological impact of your solution on individual stakeholders. Does it reduce stress? Does it increase confidence? Does it eliminate embarrassment? DataFlow discovered that their solution's emotional value - professional confidence and work-life balance - often mattered more than its technical capabilities.

SOCIAL VALUE

Social value addresses how your solution affects stakeholder relationships and organizational standing. Does it enhance collaborative capabilities? Does it improve internal service levels? Does it position adopters as innovative leaders within their organizations?

ECONOMIC VALUE

Economic value transcends simple ROI calculations to encompass career advancement potential, competitive positioning, and strategic option creation. The best offers demonstrate clear paths to promotions, market leadership, and expanded opportunities.

Risk Reversal as Value Amplification

Traditional risk mitigation focuses on reducing downside exposure through contracts and service level agreements. Value amplification approaches risk reversal as upside enhancement - making success so certain that not buying becomes the risky decision.

DataFlow transformed their offer structure by guaranteeing specific outcome achievements within defined timeframes. Instead of promising software functionality, they committed to operational transformations. "Reduce reporting cycle time by 75% within ninety days or we'll refund your investment and pay for competitive solution implementation."

This guarantee shifted risk from customer to vendor while dramatically increasing perceived value. Prospects no longer evaluated whether the solution might work - they evaluated whether they could afford to miss guaranteed outcomes.

Implementation as Value Delivery

Most companies treat implementation as a necessary evil following the sale. Market leaders recognize implementation as the primary value delivery mechanism that determines long-term relationship success.

The DataFlow team redesigned their onboarding process to deliver quick wins within the first thirty days, building momentum and confidence before tackling complex integration challenges. Early success created internal advocates who smoothed future adoption obstacles.

Outcome Ownership vs. Tool Provision

The most irresistible offers take responsibility for customer success rather than simply providing tools for potential success. Instead of selling software subscriptions, you're selling guaranteed outcomes.

This shift requires deeper customer understanding, more sophisticated implementation methodologies, and greater confidence in your solution's capabilities. But it also commands premium pricing, accelerates decision cycles, and creates customer relationships that competitors can't easily replicate.

When prospects evaluate your offer, they're not just buying your solution - they're buying confidence in their decision-making, insurance for their careers, and ammunition for their internal success stories. The companies that understand this multi-layered evaluation process create offers that feel less like vendor relationships and more like strategic partnerships.

Your offer becomes irresistible when saying no feels like choosing mediocrity over excellence, accepting problems over solutions, and gambling with careers over investing in success.

The Intelligence Advantage: Turning Insights into Revenue

What if the difference between your most successful deals and your biggest losses came down to a single conversation you never had?

That realization hit me during a DataFlow post-mortem analysis. Their most lucrative customer relationships all shared one characteristic: comprehensive baseline measurements before implementation, followed by rigorous outcome tracking after deployment. Their least successful engagements? They skipped the measurement phase and jumped straight into solution delivery.

The intelligence advantage isn't about having better data - it's about using customer insights as a revenue generation system that compounds over time.

Calculate Impact Together

The most powerful sales tool isn't a presentation deck or demo environment - it's a collaborative calculator where you and your customer quantify transformation potential together. When prospects participate in building their own business case, they become invested in the outcomes rather than skeptical of your promises.

During customer interviews, we learned that DataFlow's champions became strongest advocates when they co-created ROI projections with the sales team. Instead of being presented with generic case studies, they built custom models reflecting their specific operational challenges and improvement opportunities.

This collaborative approach transforms vendor-customer dynamics. You no longer pitch solutions - you partner on strategic analysis. The customer doesn't evaluate your claims - they validate their projections.

Before and After Snapshots

Documentation becomes your competitive weapon when you systematically capture baseline conditions before implementation, then measure actual improvements twelve months later. These verified transformations become irrefutable proof points that eliminate skepticism in future sales conversations.

One DataFlow customer reduced monthly reporting cycle time from 240 hours to forty-five while improving data accuracy from 73% to 97%. Those numbers weren't marketing claims - they were jointly verified measurements that became case study gold.

But measurement sophistication varies by stakeholder. Financial executives want quantified business impact: revenue growth, cost reduction, efficiency gains, risk mitigation value. Operational leaders focus on process improvements: time savings, error reduction, workflow optimization, resource allocation enhancement.

Technical stakeholders evaluate performance metrics: system reliability, processing speed, integration complexity, security compliance. End users measure experience improvements: ease of use, feature accessibility, training requirements, daily workflow impact.

Role-Based Testimonials as Credibility Multipliers

Generic customer testimonials waste valuable social proof opportunities. The most persuasive references speak directly to specific stakeholder concerns from peers facing identical challenges.

A CFO evaluating your solution doesn't care about technical architecture praise from IT directors. They want to hear from other CFOs about budget impact, ROI realization, and strategic value creation. An operations manager needs validation from operational peers about implementation complexity and change management success.

DataFlow transformed their reference strategy by creating stakeholder-specific testimonial libraries. Champions could share workflow transformation stories with fellow analysts. Decision-makers could present strategic outcome summaries to other executives. Each stakeholder received peer validation for their specific evaluation criteria.

Economic Buyer Intelligence

Understanding who controls budget approval versus who influences spending decisions prevents countless deal failures. The person signing contracts isn't always the person making purchasing decisions, and the person making decisions isn't always the person evaluating solutions.

Map the complete approval hierarchy: Who has formal authority? Who has informal influence? What approval processes must be followed? Which stakeholders can accelerate decisions, and which can delay them indefinitely?

During one DataFlow evaluation, the IT director had enthusiastically endorsed their solution, but the deal stalled mysteriously. Investigation revealed that the CFO, never mentioned in previous conversations, required additional risk assessment documentation for any technology investment exceeding $100,000. Six weeks of delay could have been avoided with proper economic buyer mapping.

Influence Architecture Understanding

Beyond formal reporting structures, successful deal navigation requires understanding informal influence networks within target organizations. Who do decision-makers consult before approving major investments? Which relationships can accelerate internal consensus-building?

Sometimes the most influential person in your deal is someone you've never met: a trusted advisor, board member, or department head whose opinion carries disproportionate weight with your primary contacts.

The DataFlow team learned to ask champions directly: "Who else's opinion does your CEO typically seek before approving investments like this?" These conversations revealed informal advisors who could become powerful advocates or dangerous blockers.

Continuous Intelligence Gathering

Customer intelligence gathering shouldn't end with contract signature - it should intensify during implementation and expand throughout the relationship lifecycle. Post-implementation insights become pre-sales intelligence for future opportunities.

Successful customers become your best sales team when they share specific improvement metrics with peer organizations. Their transformation stories become your most compelling marketing content. Their implementation lessons become your competitive differentiation in subsequent deals.

The companies that master customer intelligence don't just sell solutions - they build learning systems that continuously improve their value proposition, refine their ideal customer profile, and accelerate their growth trajectory.

From Customer Clarity to Market Dominance

The transformation at DataFlow Solutions didn't happen overnight, but it was unmistakable. Within eighteen months, they evolved from a struggling software vendor competing on features to a strategic partner commanding premium prices for guaranteed outcomes. Their sales team stopped chasing every lead and started attracting ideal customers who closed faster and stayed longer.

This metamorphosis began with a fundamental shift in perspective: understanding that your ideal customer isn't about who you want to serve - it's about who you can serve most effectively. When you truly understand the intersection between your capabilities and your customer's deepest needs, everything else becomes tactical execution.

The framework we've explored transcends traditional customer profiling because it addresses the full complexity of modern B2B purchasing. You're not just identifying company characteristics - you're mapping human motivations, organizational dynamics, and decision-making psychology that determine whether prospects become advocates or cautionary tales.

Remember the Pain Equation: Corporate Pain + Personal Pain = Buying Urgency. Your solution must address both operational challenges and individual stakeholder concerns. Miss either dimension, and your perfectly logical value proposition becomes irrelevant to actual decision-making.

The Total Cost Reality framework protects you from the dangerous misconception that price is your primary competitive battleground. When prospects understand the complete investment equation - time, risk, reputation, opportunity cost, and political capital - your subscription fee becomes the smallest line item in their evaluation.

Most importantly, recognize that Customer understanding is a dynamic capability, not a static achievement. Markets evolve, competitive landscapes shift, and customer priorities change. The companies that maintain growth momentum treat customer intelligence as an ongoing strategic discipline rather than a one-time research project.

Your ideal customer profile becomes your strategic compass, guiding product development decisions, marketing investment allocation, sales team hiring priorities, and partnership evaluation criteria. When every organizational function aligns around serving specific customer segments optimally, you create competitive advantages that transcend individual product features or pricing strategies.

The DataFlow team discovered that knowing their customers intimately didn't just improve their sales results - it transformed their entire business model. They moved from reactive problem-solving to proactive value creation, from vendor relationships to strategic partnerships, from competing on features to owning outcomes.

This level of customer intimacy requires commitment, curiosity, and systematic investigation. But the payoff extends far beyond sales metrics to encompass organizational confidence, strategic clarity, and sustainable competitive positioning.

Five Actions to Transform Your Customer Understanding

1. Conduct the Champion Audit

Interview your top five customers' primary champions within the next thirty days. Ask them specifically: "What was happening in your professional life that made solving this problem urgent?" and "How has this solution affected your career trajectory?" Document corporate and personal benefits they've realized. These insights will revolutionize your value proposition and sales conversations.

2. Map Your Buying Committee Architecture

Create a visual diagram of the complete decision-making structure for your three most recent deals. Include not only participants but influencers, blockers, and approval authorities. Identify who joined conversations at which stages and what concerns each stakeholder raised. This intelligence becomes your playbook for future deal navigation.

3. Calculate Total Cost Reality

Build a comprehensive cost model that includes customer time investment, risk exposure, reputation stakes, opportunity costs, and political capital required for your solution adoption. Present this analysis to prospects as investment optimization rather than price justification. Most competitors ignore these hidden costs, giving you massive differentiation opportunities.

4. Establish Baseline Measurement Systems

Implement a process for capturing quantified "before" snapshots of customer conditions prior to implementation, then track specific improvements six and twelve months later. Create stakeholder-specific measurement frameworks that matter to each persona: CFOs get financial impact, operations leaders get efficiency gains, end users get experience improvements.

5. Launch Systematic Intelligence Gathering

Schedule quarterly interviews with existing customers to understand how their challenges, priorities, and market conditions are evolving. Ask about new competitors, changing regulations, emerging technologies, and strategic initiatives that could create future opportunities. This ongoing intelligence becomes your early warning system for market shifts and product development priorities.

Your journey toward customer mastery begins with a single conversation, but it never truly ends. Each interaction deepens your understanding, each implementation teaches valuable lessons, and each success story becomes ammunition for future growth.

The companies that dominate their markets don't just know their customers - they understand them so completely that buying becomes inevitable, retention becomes automatic, and advocacy becomes natural.

TEMPLATES

06

CHAPTER

Getting the Right People in the Right Jobs

Marcus sat in his conference room looking at the numbers. He was the CTO of a growing fintech startup, and things weren't going well. He'd hired 40% more people, but somehow his team was getting less done. They were spending money like crazy, but their product releases kept getting delayed. Sound familiar?

Marcus made the same mistake lots of tech leaders make. He thought hiring more people would automatically fix his problems. He'd hired smart people from good universities and big companies. But something was wrong. The wake-up call came from his daughter, who played high school soccer. She mentioned how her coach spent three weeks figuring out who should play which position before the season started.

"You have to get the right people on the bus first," as Jim Collins said. But here's what most leaders miss - it's not just about getting talented people. It's about knowing exactly where each person should sit and why they belong there.

People are your most valuable asset. Companies say this all the time, but they don't really mean it. Great companies invest time in understanding their workforce. They have better reputations, move faster when opportunities come up, and make more money. The numbers don't lie - while only 23% of employees worldwide care about their jobs, the best companies get 70% of their people engaged.

Here's a scary fact: Over 50% of employees in tech aren't happy in their current roles. That means they're not doing their best work. Even worse, 17% are actively trying to hurt their companies. Let that sink in, 17% are actively trying to hurt their current employer. These aren't just numbers - they're millions of talented people whose skills are wasted because their companies put them in the wrong jobs.

The money impact is huge. Companies with engaged employees make 23% more profit. But most organizations obsess over processes and products while treating people like replaceable parts. This backwards thinking is why so many promising companies struggle.

The best organizations work like championship sports teams. A soccer coach wouldn't put their fastest player in goal or their smartest player on the wing. Great business leaders know that every role needs specific skills and personality traits. A brilliant software architect might fail in customer service, while a great customer success manager could crash in high-pressure sales.

The challenge isn't finding talented people - it's figuring out where they'll do their best work. This means looking deeper than just qualifications. You need to understand what really drives performance. Is your job description clear enough to attract the right people while scaring away the wrong ones? Do you really know what skills the job needs? More importantly, do you know what personality traits help someone succeed in each position?

Using experts in the field of psychology to support role description development, candidate assessment and leadership development might be the best invest you can make.

I recently met with a friend who is doing pilot assessments for airlines. She has a university degree in psychology and further certifications in advanced psychological diagnostics. As you can imagine, hiring pilots doesn't leave any room for failure. When I discussed with her how candidate assessment is done in the tech industry, she was truly shocked. She couldn't believe that even multi-billion-dollar companies are not relying on experts for candidate assessment, leadership hiring and people development.

Marcus eventually fixed his engineering team by hiring an external expert and taking a systematic approach. Together they discovered that his best developers shared certain traits: they wanted autonomy, liked working with new technologies, and did well when given clear goals without micromanagement. Using these insights, he restructured his teams, developed new role requirements and changed how he hired. Within six months, productivity jumped 35%, and employee satisfaction hit company records.

The secret wasn't only hiring better people - it was better understanding the people he already had, hiring the right personality types for any given role and making sure they were set up to win.

Writing Job Descriptions That Work

Imagine walking into a restaurant where the menu just says "food" without describing any dishes. You'd probably leave, confused and frustrated. Yet this happens every day in corporate hiring, where generic job descriptions attract generic candidates who deliver generic results.

Sarah was VP of Marketing at a fast-growing SaaS company. She needed to expand her team quickly, so she posted a job for a "Marketing Specialist" with the usual list: "develop marketing strategies, manage campaigns, analyze performance metrics, work with sales team." This description could apply to any marketing job at any company. After interviewing dozens of people, she hired someone with great credentials and ten years of experience.

Six months later, that hire was struggling. Despite all that experience, they didn't have expertise in the specific areas Sarah's company needed most. The problem wasn't the person - it was the process. Sarah hired a generalist when she needed a specialist, because she wasn't clear about what success looked like.

Great organizations approach job descriptions differently. They know that hiring the best person for any position requires laser focus on what that position involves. This means describing daily tasks precisely, identifying the specific metrics that measure success, and explaining exactly how this role helps the company win.

Even more important - and mostly ignored - is defining the personality traits needed for success. Skills can be taught; personality runs much deeper. When you're vague about what the job needs, you end up with talented generalists who lack specialized expertise in the areas that matter.

One of my client companies changed their marketing results by getting forensic about job descriptions. Instead of generic "marketing" positions, they created specific specialist roles with crystal-clear requirements. Their marketing team now includes a **tech stack expert** whose only job is constantly improving tools and methods to increase click-through rates while reducing cost per click. This person's goal is simple: build the best marketing technology setup possible. Their metrics include cost per click and click-through rates. Their objective: "Reduce cost per click by 20% while increasing click-through rate by 18%."

And they didn't stop at metrics. They identified the specific personality traits this role needs: curiosity, love of change, enthusiasm for continuous learning, and analytical thinking. They look for someone who focuses on achieving goals rather than avoiding problems, pays attention to details, and follows procedures. They know this person will work closely with SEO experts and social media specialists, so collaboration skills matter a lot.

Their recruiting reflects this precision. They target universities and research teams where they're likely to find candidates with the right technical foundation. When attracting candidates, they lead with something irresistible: "You'll develop and evolve the most sophisticated tech stack in the world, and nobody will tell you how to do it." For someone with the right personality, this is the ultimate professional challenge.

Their management approach is equally specific. This role needs freedom and autonomy - micromanagement would kill it. The right candidate thrives when given clear objectives and space to innovate. Understanding these dynamics from the start prevents the mismatched expectations that destroy otherwise good hires.

This level of precision becomes even more important when hiring managers. Leadership roles amplify good and bad traits throughout the organization. The worst thing you can do is promote someone with strong individual skills but completely wrong personality traits for leading others. The most dangerous traits in leadership include selfishness, ego-driven behavior, and excessive focus on details. These people focus on themselves rather than others, get lost in details rather than seeing the big picture, and spend time avoiding problems rather than solving them.

Promoting someone with these traits into leadership almost guarantees team problems and organizational damage. The impact spreads like a virus, affecting not just their direct reports but everyone who works with that team. The best companies prioritize personality assessment for leadership roles, looking for people who focus on solving problems, care about people rather than just tasks, and think big picture rather than getting stuck in details.

The difference between precise and vague job descriptions isn't just academic - it determines whether you attract people who can excel or just survive.

Looking Beyond the Resume

Most hiring decisions are made within the first seven minutes of an interview, but the traits that predict long-term success often take months to show up. This disconnect explains why so many perfect-on-paper hires fail while others exceed expectations despite modest credentials.

The impact of having the right people in the right roles is so huge that I'm shocked how primitive most hiring remains. Generic job descriptions, shallow understanding of what roles need, and minimal thought about how positions fit within the bigger picture aren't exceptions - they're normal. We're making million-dollar decisions based on gut feelings and thirty-minute conversations.

Think about football. Imagine if coaches picked players based only on athletic ability without considering what position they'd play. A brilliant goalkeeper might have great reflexes and decision-making but fail completely as a striker. An outstanding striker's aggressive, goal-focused mindset could be terrible for defense. Each position needs different capabilities, and the best coaches understand these details.

The best companies work with similar sophistication when evaluating role fit. They've spent time understanding exactly what each area needs for success. They know why specific skills matter, what personality traits enable peak performance, and how different roles work together to create success. In these organizations, a position only gets approved after these requirements are defined clearly.

The assessment process itself needs expertise that most companies lack. Outstanding organizations involve highly trained specialists with backgrounds in psychology or related fields who can accurately evaluate personality traits and role compatibility. These aren't HR generalists doing standard interviews - they're experts who understand the subtle behavioral patterns that predict success or failure.

I experienced this sophistication during an interview for a senior leadership position at an international tech company. I met Francesco, a charismatic guy who apologized in advance for what he called a "dentist appointment" experience. His assessment involved a complex role-playing scenario where I had to make a senior leadership decision under pressure. After I explained my choice, Francesco systematically challenged my reasoning and questioned my logic. It was intense and frankly uncomfortable.

What made this assessment brilliant wasn't the scenario itself - it was Francesco's explanation afterward. The exercise wasn't designed to evaluate my decision-making ability, which could be tested other ways. Instead, it measured how I responded to having my judgment challenged by someone in authority. Did I get defensive? Did I crumble under pressure? Did I stay confident while remaining open to other perspectives? These behavioral responses predicted far more about my leadership potential than any traditional interview question.

This kind of sophisticated personality assessment is rare in hiring and almost never used in promotions. Yet these psychological patterns determine whether someone will succeed or struggle in leadership roles. Technical skills and past performance give incomplete pictures of future success, especially when the new role is significantly different from previous positions.

The football team demonstrates systematic assessment in action. Each player's role is clearly defined: strikers focus on scoring, midfielders control game flow, defenders protect against threats. The coach understands each position's requirements and evaluates players accordingly. They wouldn't judge a defender's performance using striker metrics or expect a midfielder to excel at goalkeeper responsibilities.

Similarly, exceptional organizations develop position-specific assessment criteria that go far beyond generic frameworks. They understand that successful sales leaders need different traits than engineering managers, that customer success roles need different capabilities than product development positions, and that what makes someone exceptional as an individual contributor might make them toxic as a team leader.

The assessment process must also consider team dynamics and cultural fit. A brilliant individual whose working style clashes with the existing team can destroy more value than they create. This requires understanding not just the candidate's capabilities but how those capabilities interact with current team members' strengths and weaknesses.

Smart companies have learned that hiring decisions have exponential impact. One exceptional hire in a key position can elevate an entire team's performance, while one poor hire can create problems that last for years. Given these stakes, investing in sophisticated assessment processes isn't just wise - it's essential for sustainable growth.

The goal isn't perfection - it's dramatically improving the odds of matching people with roles where they can excel while contributing to organizational success.

When Great People Meet Great Systems

Here's something that keeps exceptional leaders awake at night: hiring perfectly matched people for their roles is only half the battle. The other half - often harder - involves creating an environment where those people can perform at their peak.

Imagine recruiting a Formula One driver and then asking them to race in a go-kart with worn tires and a broken engine. That's what happens when organizations hire talented people but fail to provide the tools, processes, and support systems necessary for success. Even the most capable people get frustrated and check out when their environment limits their potential.

Less than 50% of employees know what's expected of them at work. Half of your workforce operates without clear understanding of their responsibilities, success metrics, or how their efforts contribute to company goals. Only 30% feel aligned with their company's vision and mission. These aren't engagement problems - they're leadership failures that handicap otherwise capable people.

Great people need great systems to achieve exceptional results. This means providing cutting-edge tools that amplify their capabilities rather than creating friction. It means designing processes that enhance efficiency rather than bureaucratic obstacles that slow progress. Most importantly, it means establishing crystal-clear goals and expectations, so people understand exactly what success looks like.

But here's where many organizations stumble: they focus on the technical infrastructure while neglecting the human infrastructure. The biggest risk to employee performance isn't outdated software or inefficient workflows - it's incompetent or toxic leadership. Poor leaders create environments where even exceptional people struggle to succeed.

I've seen this repeatedly throughout my career. One particularly memorable example involved working with a manager who had earned multiple promotions and enjoyed widespread organizational respect. To senior leadership, she appeared competent and results driven. However, her actual leadership style created a culture of fear and blame-shifting that poisoned everything around her.

This manager had one focus: making herself look good to senior leadership, regardless of the cost to her team or other departments. She actively hunted for mistakes made by others, within her team and in adjacent groups. Instead of offering help when she found problems, she immediately escalated these findings to executives, positioning herself as the vigilant guardian of quality standards.

Her team lived in constant stress, knowing that any mistake would be used against them. People began avoiding risks, sharing less information, and focusing more on self-protection than innovation. The broader organization suffered as teams became reluctant to collaborate, fearing that any shared challenges would be weaponized against them. What appeared from above as strong performance management was systematic destruction of trust and psychological safety.

The ripple effects extended far beyond her direct reports. Adjacent teams modified their behavior to avoid her scrutiny, leading to less transparency and reduced cross-functional collaboration. Talented people began requesting transfers or leaving the company entirely, not because they couldn't do the work, but because the environment made excellent work impossible.

This scenario shows why leadership quality is the most critical factor in employee success. Tools and processes matter, but they pale compared to the leadership environment that either unleashes or constrains human potential. Toxic leaders don't just limit their direct reports - they create organizational cancer that spreads throughout interconnected teams.

Exceptional organizations recognize this reality and invest accordingly. They understand that leadership development isn't a nice-to-have training program - it's the foundation that determines whether their talent investments pay off or create expensive frustration. They also implement systems to identify and address toxic leadership before it spreads throughout the organization.

Creating an environment where great people can excel requires more than eliminating negative influences. It demands proactive investment in the infrastructure of success. This includes providing state-of-the-art tools that enhance rather than hinder productivity. It means designing workflows that eliminate unnecessary friction while maintaining appropriate quality controls. Most importantly, it requires leaders who understand their primary job: removing obstacles so their people can focus on creating value.

The performance equation is simple: **great people + great systems = exceptional results**. But achieving this requires deliberate attention to both sides. You can't compensate for poor systems with extraordinary people, nor can excellent systems overcome the wrong people in key positions.

Smart leaders audit both elements regularly, asking whether their people have everything they need to succeed and whether any environmental factors are constraining performance unnecessarily.

Turning Good into Great

There's a moment in every high-performing organization when you realize something: the companies that consistently beat their competitors aren't necessarily those with the most talented people - they're the ones that most effectively develop the talent they have.

Most organizations approach employee development like they're checking boxes. They deploy generic training programs through online modules or weekend workshops, assuming exposure equals transformation. Meanwhile, the best companies understand a fundamental truth: development isn't an event; it's an ongoing process that requires dedicated expertise and systematic attention.

The difference shows up in investment patterns. Exceptional organizations hire dedicated coaches who provide one-on-one development for leaders, help managers during coaching conversations, and give regular feedback to executive teams about organizational health. These aren't HR generalists wearing multiple hats - they're specialists whose only focus is unlocking human potential.

Here's what separates truly excellent companies from the merely good ones: they create feedback loops that drive improvement. Anonymous employee surveys become powerful diagnostic tools when organizations commit to acting on what they learn. The magic happens not in collecting data but in what leaders do with that information.

I saw this transformation while working for a company that did comprehensive employee engagement surveys twice a year. What made their approach extraordinary wasn't the survey itself - it was what happened afterward. Each manager had to present their team's results back to their people, including how their leadership effectiveness compared to company averages. Imagine the courage required for a manager to stand before their team and acknowledge that engagement scores and satisfaction with their leadership fell below organizational standards.

The process didn't stop with acknowledgment. Each manager also had to present a detailed action plan for improvement, developed with internal leadership coaches. These weren't vague commitments to "communicate better" or "be more supportive." They were specific, measurable changes with clear timelines and accountability mechanisms.

The coaching support proved crucial. Internal experts helped managers understand what was driving their team's feedback, identifying specific behaviors and patterns that needed modification. They attended team meetings and one-on-one sessions, providing real-time feedback and guidance. This wasn't theory being discussed in a conference room - it was practical application with immediate course correction when needed.

The results spoke volumes. The team I was part of saw engagement scores improve dramatically over the following year, but more importantly, our actual performance increased by about 45%. People felt heard, valued, and supported in their development. The transparency created trust, the coaching provided tools for improvement, and the accountability ensured that changes happened rather than being forgotten after the initial presentation.

This approach worked because it addressed the fundamental challenge in most development efforts: the gap between knowing what to do and doing it consistently. Most managers understand theoretically that they should provide better feedback, communicate more clearly, and support their people's growth. The challenge lies in translating this knowledge into daily behaviors, especially under pressure.

Expert coaching bridges this gap by providing ongoing support during real situations. Instead of learning about leadership in a classroom, managers receive guidance while leading. They get immediate feedback on their communication style during difficult conversations, support in navigating team conflicts, and help recognizing when their natural tendencies might be counterproductive.

The best coaching also helps leaders understand their blind spots - the unconscious patterns that limit their effectiveness. We all have default behaviors that serve us well in some situations while creating problems in others. Self-awareness is the starting point for growth, but it requires external perspective to identify patterns we can't see ourselves.

Outstanding organizations also recognize that development must be continuous rather than one-time events. Training creates temporary enthusiasm but rarely produces lasting change. Sustainable improvement requires ongoing reinforcement, practice opportunities, and gradual skill building over time.

The companies that excel in this area treat development as a competitive advantage rather than a cost center. They understand that their ability to grow and evolve their people directly correlates with their ability to adapt to changing market conditions and capitalize on new opportunities. In rapidly evolving industries like technology, this capability often determines which companies thrive and which struggle to remain relevant.

Investment in people development also pays dividends in retention and engagement. When employees feel that their organization is genuinely committed to their growth, they become more invested in contributing to organizational success. The best people want to work for companies that will help them become even better versions of themselves.

When Individual Excellence Meets Team Dynamics

You can put together the most talented individuals in the world and still create a dysfunctional team. This paradox haunts organizations that focus only on individual capabilities while ignoring the psychological and behavioral dynamics that determine how people work together.

Team formation is one of the most underestimated skills in leadership, yet it often determines whether organizations achieve breakthrough results or struggle with internal friction. The challenge goes beyond matching skills to requirements - it requires understanding how different personality types interact, complement each other's strengths, and potentially create destructive conflicts.

Some teams work independently, with minimal collaboration required between members. In these situations, team dynamics matter less than individual performance. But when team success depends on close collaboration, shared decision-making, and coordinated execution, understanding personality interactions becomes critical. You can have the most capable individuals in the world forming a low-performing team simply because their working styles clash rather than complement.

Patrick Lencioni's work *The Five Dysfunctions of a Team* shows this challenge by identifying the behavioral patterns that undermine team effectiveness. His research reveals that team dysfunction rarely stems from lack of talent or inadequate resources - it emerges from interpersonal dynamics that prevent people from working together effectively.

The foundation of exceptional teams starts with psychological safety, where team members feel secure enough to be vulnerable, admit mistakes, and engage in productive conflict about ideas rather than personalities. Without this foundation, even brilliant people waste energy on self-protection instead of focusing on results. They avoid taking risks, withhold important information, and prioritize looking good over being effective.

Understanding the personality frameworks we've discussed becomes particularly valuable in team formation. Remember the color-coded behavior types that help predict how people respond to stress, communicate, and what motivates them? **Red personalities** (dominant and results-oriented) often clash with **green personalities** (stable and relationship-focused) because their natural approaches to problem-solving differ dramatically. Reds want to move quickly and make decisions, while greens prefer to build consensus and consider all perspectives.

However, this potential conflict can become a powerful advantage when leaders understand how to harness these differences. Red team members drive urgency and results focus, while green members ensure that decisions consider long-term implications and team cohesion. The key lies in establishing team norms that leverage both perspectives rather than allowing them to create gridlock.

Similarly, **blue personalities** (analytical and detail-oriented) can frustrate **yellow personalities** (inspiring and people-focused) with their methodical approach to decision-making. Yellows want to explore possibilities and move quickly, while blues need time to analyze data and consider potential risks. Yet teams that successfully integrate both perspectives often make better decisions because they balance innovation with careful analysis.

The most effective team leaders act like orchestra conductors, understanding each team member's natural "instrument" and knowing when to feature different capabilities. They recognize that diversity of thinking styles creates better outcomes, but only when that diversity is orchestrated rather than allowed to create chaos.

Team formation also requires considering how roles interconnect and depend on each other. Just as a football team needs players who understand not only their position but how their performance affects teammates, business teams perform best when members understand their interdependencies. The marketing team's messaging decisions impact the sales team's effectiveness. The engineering team's architecture choices influence the customer success team's ability to solve problems quickly.

Exceptional leaders map these interconnections and ensure team members understand how their individual success contributes to collective achievement. They also identify potential friction points where different roles might have competing priorities and establish clear protocols for resolving these tensions constructively.

The goal isn't eliminating all conflict - healthy teams engage in passionate debates about ideas while maintaining respect for individuals. The challenge is creating an environment where conflict becomes productive rather than destructive, where people challenge approaches without attacking character, and where diverse perspectives enhance rather than undermine decision-making.

Building exceptional teams requires intentional design rather than hoping talented people will naturally collaborate effectively. It demands understanding individual capabilities and interpersonal dynamics, then creating the structures and norms that allow both to flourish.

Your Action Plan

The distance between understanding these principles and implementing them successfully lies in your willingness to take specific, measurable action. Here are five steps that will immediately improve your organization's approach to employee selection and team formation:

Involve an Expert with a Background in Psychology

Check whether you have an expert with a background in behavioral psychology within your organization. If you can't find someone with the right expertise within your company, find an external specialist. Long term I recommend to hire an absolute rock star and make that person part of your strategic leadership team.

Do a Role Description Audit

Together with your internal or external expert, review every job description in your organization and grade them on specificity. Do they clearly define day-to-day responsibilities, success metrics, and required personality traits? Create detailed role profiles for your three most critical positions, including specific KPIs, personality requirements, and team interaction expectations. Be very clear on whether a role requires someone that is more strategic or an executer. Start with your most senior leadership role descriptions and work your way downwards. Set a deadline to complete at least your senior leadership role descriptions within thirty days.

Use Personality-Based Assessment for Your Next Three Hires

Develop together with your expert position-specific interview scenarios that reveal how candidates respond to the types of challenges they'll face in your environment. Document these scenarios and train your hiring managers to recognize the behavioral patterns that predict success for a specific role.

Set Up a Team Chemistry Review Process

Map the personality types within your three most important teams using a consistent framework. Identify potential friction points between different behavioral styles and establish team norms that leverage differences rather than allowing them to create conflict. Schedule quarterly team dynamics discussions to address emerging challenges before they become problems.

Set Up a Six-Month Development Check-In System

Implement anonymous feedback mechanisms that allow team members to provide honest input about leadership effectiveness, team dynamics, and organizational support. Require managers to present results back to their teams along with specific improvement plans that are developed with your expert. Provide coaching support to help leaders translate feedback into behavioral changes.

TEMPLATES

The organizations that consistently outperform their competitors understand a simple truth: success flows from getting the right people in the right roles, then creating an environment where they can do their best work together. Your competitive advantage lies not just in the talent you attract, but in how effectively you develop and deploy that talent toward shared goals.

These strategies provide a roadmap, but implementation requires commitment to sustained effort rather than quick fixes. Start with one area where you can make immediate progress, then systematically expand your approach as you build confidence and capability.

Remember Marcus from our opening story? His transformation didn't happen overnight, but within six months of implementing these principles, his engineering organization became a model of productivity and engagement. The same potential exists within your organization - it simply requires the discipline to treat people with the same rigor you apply to money.

Your people are waiting for you to unlock their potential. The question isn't whether they're capable of exceptional performance - it's whether you're committed to creating the conditions where that performance can flourish.

07

CHAPTER

Designing an Agile Organization

I remember an awkward situation 2 years back in Rome. Fabio, CEO of an Italian tech company, stared at the numbers on the big screen. Revenue was flat. Customer complaints had tripled. His once-nimble startup, now with 2,500 people across fourteen countries, felt like a giant stuck in mud. The irony hit him hard - the company that built its reputation on fast innovation could no longer move quickly enough to compete with startups or match the resources of big enterprises.

"How did we get here?" he asked his leadership team, knowing the answer would hurt.

The silence stretched until his CTO, Davide, spoke up. "We chose control over speed. Every decision needs six approvals. Our development cycles went from weeks to quarters. We became what we used to disrupt."

Fabio's story plays out in boardrooms across the tech sector. The bigger an organization gets, the more important it becomes to stay efficient and effective. Yet most large organizations have become exactly what Fabio's company faced - slow, heavy giants that can't adapt to changing conditions and waste tremendous resources through bureaucratic friction.

The old organizational structures that worked in predictable markets now feel like straitjackets in times of constant change. Your company likely shows similar symptoms: long approval chains, duplicated work across departments, teams that pass work around instead of owning results, and middle management layers that add oversight but little value.

Many organizations are racing toward agility as the solution, but few understand what enterprise agility means or how to implement it successfully. Recent research shows the power of true agile transformation - companies that get it right see significant improvements across multiple areas of performance. But the key word here is "right."

Enterprise agility isn't about implementing Scrum ceremonies in a few software teams or hanging Kanban boards in hallways. It's a fundamental rethinking of how work flows through your organization, how decisions get made, and how value reaches your customers. It's about creating what researchers call an "agile impact engine" - a system where improved customer satisfaction, better employee engagement, and superior operational performance reinforce each other to drive measurable financial results.

Think of agility as your organization's ability to sense and respond to change faster than the rate of change itself. In the software industry, where tech shifts can make entire business models obsolete overnight, this isn't a nice-to-have capability - it's survival.

Here's what most executives miss: agility and scale aren't opposites. You don't have to sacrifice stability for speed or trade control for flexibility. Truly agile organizations combine both through the "stable core, dynamic edge" principle. They maintain a strong backbone that provides stability while enabling rapid changes to teams, priorities, and strategies in response to market signals.

This backbone combines structural stability - your standard operating procedures, quality gates, and governance frameworks - with cultural stability through shared purpose, direction, and values. This foundation then supports dynamic capabilities that allow fluid changes to strategy, team composition, and resource allocation without losing direction.

The question isn't whether your organization needs to become more agile. In today's tech business landscape, that's already been decided for you. The question is whether you'll approach this transformation strategically or stumble through it reactively.

Before looking at organizational structures and methods, we need to examine a more fundamental question that will determine the success or failure of any agility effort: What is your organization truly built for?

What Are You Really Optimized for?

Step back from your daily operations and honestly assess where your organization focuses its energy. Is your company built around internal needs - maximum control and minimum cost - or is it centered around what your customers and employees need?

This isn't theoretical. The answer shows up in how your people spend their time, where your meetings focus, and what gets measured and rewarded. In traditionally structured organizations, vast amounts of energy get consumed by internal coordination, approval processes, and political maneuvering. People spend more time managing up and across than delivering value down to customers. Forecasting becomes the center of attention and dictates the company's rhythm.

Look at where your teams invest their hours. How much time goes to creating reports for other internal teams versus improving customer experiences? How many meetings focus on resource allocation disputes versus outcomes and innovation? How often do your best people get pulled into "alignment" sessions instead of solving customer problems?

Enterprise agility fundamentally shifts this equation. It's a way of scaling agile methods beyond isolated functional teams to create systematic customer obsession throughout your organization. When implemented successfully, agile transformation efforts consistently increase customer satisfaction, reduce operating costs, and create genuine employee engagement - not the surface-level engagement measured by annual surveys, but the deep commitment that emerges when people see their work directly impacting customers.

The most successful agile transformations are driven by a North Star vision we worked on earlier in chapter 4. "North Star" - a shared purpose and vision that centers entirely around customer needs. Amazon's North Star, "We seek to be Earth's most customer-centric company," isn't marketing speak. It's a decision-making framework that informs every choice, from technical architecture to hiring practices.

Your North Star becomes essential during an agile transformation because it provides the language and logic for independent decision-making. When teams understand the ultimate customer outcome they're serving, they can make rapid choices without escalating everything up the management chain. The North Star doesn't replace leadership; it enables distributed leadership at every level.

This customer obsession represents more than a cultural shift - it's a competitive necessity. Using enterprise agility to meet rapidly changing customer needs consistently results in superior customer experiences. Organizations that complete successful agile transformations typically see customer satisfaction and engagement improve by ten to thirty points. This isn't marginal improvement; it's the difference between customers who tolerate your product and customers who advocate for it.

And customer focus requires more than good intentions. It demands organizational structures that support rapid response to customer feedback, development processes that deliver value in short cycles, and incentive systems that reward customer outcomes over internal metrics.

The shift starts with an uncomfortable audit of your current reality. Map the journey your customers experience when they interact with your organization. Track how long it takes for customer feedback to reach the people who can act on it. Measure the time between identifying a customer need and delivering a solution. Calculate how many internal handoffs occur before value reaches your customers. What is the customer experience when dealing with your company?

Most tech companies discover that their organizations have been built for maximum control and efficiency rather than customer value. The company's rhythm is dictated by internal reporting cycles. Action towards customers is prioritized by internal metrics. Forecast calls are more important than customer needs. Reviewing lagging KPIs in quarterly meetings is more important than discussing leading KPIs and feedback of customers. A deal for this quarter is more important than a long-term happy customer. Strong focus on functional KPIs rather than on progress towards a cross functional outcome. Release cycles align with internal planning schedules rather than market opportunities. Products get designed by committee. Features reflect internal politics more than customer needs.

Enterprise agility flips this equation. Instead of asking customers to adapt to your internal processes, you adapt your internal processes to serve customers more effectively. This shift sounds simple but requires fundamental changes to structure, process, and culture.

The transformation begins with accepting that your current organizational design - regardless of how successful it's been historically - may be the primary thing preventing your next level of growth. The structures that got you here won't get you there.

The Matrix Trap: When Control Becomes Chaos

Imagine this scenario: Your lead software architect gets conflicting priorities from three different managers. The product manager wants a security feature delivered by month-end. The department head demands focus on technical debt reduction. The project manager insists on meeting the quarterly roadmap commitments. Each manager believes their priority takes precedence. Your architect spends Tuesday morning in meetings trying to negotiate these competing demands instead of solving technical challenges.

Or take the following scenario: Your division lead gets conflicting goals from two different C-Suite executives. One is pushing to invest time, resource and money to launch of a new solution that would drive future profits. The other demands immediate increase in profits by focusing on legacy cash cow solutions.

Welcome to the matrix organization - the dominant structural pattern in most established companies and often the biggest barrier to agility.

Matrix organizations started in the 1950s aerospace industry, where complex projects required coordination across multiple engineering disciplines. The concept seemed logical: combine the depth of functional expertise with the focus of project management. People would report to their functional manager (ensuring skill development) and project managers (ensuring deliverable completion).

This dual-reporting structure spawned numerous variations. "Strong" matrix organizations where project managers hold primary authority. "Weak" matrices where functional managers dominate. "Product-oriented" matrices that attempt to balance both. Despite these variations, they all operate on the same fundamental principle: outputs are fixed, timing is planned, and resources become variables adjusted to meet predetermined requirements and schedules.

Think about your company's consultant and contractor expenses. That variable resource pool represents the matrix mindset in action - we fix the scope and timeline, then adjust people and budget to fit the plan.

Matrix structures initially created a sense of enhanced control. More reporting meant better oversight, right? Having multiple managers theoretically reduced execution risk by creating additional checkpoints and accountability layers. The multiplication of management roles also created appealing career mobility - plenty of fancy titles and advancement opportunities within the management hierarchy.

Warren Bennis captured the challenge perfectly: "Success in management requires learning as fast as the world is changing." Matrix organizations, however, optimize for stability over learning speed.

The matrix approach generates predictable side effects that cripple organizational agility. First, it creates internal politics exponentially. More managers create more distinct objectives that rarely align perfectly.

Teams find themselves navigating competing priorities, conflicting success metrics, and resource allocation battles. Decision-making becomes a negotiation process rather than a value-creation process.

Second, matrix structures dilute accountability through diffused responsibility. When something goes wrong, there's always another department, function, or manager to blame. Teams don't own outcomes; they own activities. Budget management happens "from above" based on departmental allocations rather than product strategy. People become accountable for completing tasks, not delivering value.

This accountability diffusion creates the "hamster wheel effect." People work hard, attend meetings, complete assignments, but lose sight of how their efforts connect to outcomes and customer value. They feel busy but not productive, active but not impactful.

Third, matrix organizations tend to overvalue management while undervaluing creation.

This logic reveals a fundamental misunderstanding of value creation in technology companies. The perceived value lies in management, coordination and optimization, not in customer experience and competitive advantage. Even when innovation and customer experience ensure company survival, organizations treat these capabilities as commodities to be managed rather than competencies to be developed.

The matrix mindset assumes that value comes from optimizing resource allocation and coordinating handoffs between specialized functions. In stable, predictable environments with well-understood requirements, this approach can work effectively. But tech markets are neither stable nor predictable.

When market conditions shift rapidly, market requirements evolve continuously, and project outcomes become inherently uncertain, matrix structures become organizational anchors rather than enablers. The time required to coordinate across functions, negotiate resource conflicts, and align competing priorities often exceeds the window of market opportunity.

Imagine what happens when your organization encounters a significant competitive threat or market opportunity. How long does it take to assemble the right team? How many approval cycles are required to reallocate resources? How many meetings must occur before decisions get made and implemented?

Matrix organizations excel at managing complexity but struggle with adapting to change. They're built for efficiency in stable conditions, not effectiveness in dynamic environments. The very characteristics that made them successful - specialization, coordination, and control - become liabilities when speed and adaptability matter more than optimization and oversight.

The irony is that many tech companies recognize these limitations but attempt to solve them with more matrix thinking. They add project management offices to coordinate projects. They create cross-functional steering committees to align priorities. They implement enterprise resource planning systems to optimize resource allocation. Each solution adds another layer of complexity to an already complex system.

These "solutions" address symptoms rather than causes. The fundamental issue isn't coordination; it's the assumption that value comes from optimizing coordination rather than maximizing customer impact. Matrix organizations optimize for internal efficiency while markets reward external effectiveness.

The Agile Alternative: Fixed Teams, Variable Outcomes

What happens when the market becomes uncertain, your product evolves continuously, and project outcomes can't be predetermined? You need organizational structures designed for adaptability rather than predictability.

Enter the agile organization - a fundamentally different approach that flips the matrix equation. Where matrix structures fix outputs and timing while making resources variable, agile organizations fix resources and time boundaries while making outcomes variable. Instead of asking, "How many people do we need to deliver this predetermined output by this fixed date?" agile organizations ask, "What's the highest value we can deliver with this stable team in this time period?"

This shift sounds simple but represents a profound change in organizational logic. Agile organizations create smaller, stable teams - typically five to ten people maximum, often called "pizza teams" because they can be fed with two pizzas - with dramatically increased communication efficiency and reduced political overhead. These teams operate with maximum independence and autonomy while maintaining alignment with overall organizational direction.

The goal becomes creating cross-functional teams that can manage an outcome from conception to delivery across all channels. In practice, complete independence isn't always possible due to complexity or scale requirements, but the aspiration drives decisions. Teams should have all necessary skills and authority to deliver customer value without depending on other teams for routine decisions or basic capabilities.

What started in development applies for other functional areas as well. If you look at sales, marketing, professional services and customer success for example. Instead of separate functions with different and often conflicting KPIs you will see cross functional units working towards a shared goal.

Recent research demonstrates the power of this approach. Organizations that successfully implement enterprise-wide agile transformations see operational performance improvements of **30% to 50%** across metrics like speed, target achievement, and predictability. More importantly, they achieve **20% to 30%** better financial performance compared to their traditional peers.

The performance gains stem from two fundamental factors that matrix organizations struggle to achieve: enhanced visibility and dedicated focus.

Agile teams operate with much clearer visibility into both expectations and current performance. Strategy gets expressed through specific, measurable objectives and key results rather than vague departmental goals. Team-level milestones and deliverables create transparency about progress and obstacles. Real-time performance dashboards enable quick adjustments rather than quarterly course corrections.

This visibility enables rapid response to changing conditions. When teams understand their current performance and their target outcomes, they can make intelligent trade-offs without escalating decisions up management hierarchies. They can sacrifice lower-priority tasks to protect critical outcomes. They can reallocate effort based on customer feedback and local requirement. They can pivot strategies based on market signals.

The second factor - dedicated focus - eliminates the productivity drain of constant context switching that plagues matrix organizations. When team members work full-time on specific outcomes rather than splitting attention across multiple projects and priorities, individual and collective performance improve dramatically.

Dedicated teams reduce handoffs between functions, departments, and individuals. Instead of passing work from development to testing to deployment to support, teams own the entire value stream. This ownership eliminates the waiting time, communication overhead, and accountability gaps that create inefficiency in matrix structures.

A good example is the transformation of a global tech and investment group operating across thirty-two countries. Despite managing tremendous complexity - five distinct business verticals, numerous subsidiaries, and ninety different nationalities - the company maintains operational agility through what they call "decentralized but not fragmented" operations.

Their approach shows that decentralization doesn't mean chaos. Real decentralization involves a cohesive framework where autonomy and collaboration work together harmoniously. Teams have control over their actions and decisions while working together toward common goals. This enables quick responses to local market conditions and customer needs while maintaining strategic coherence.

The key insight from their experience is that agile organizations require just as much structure as matrix organizations - but the structure serves different purposes. Matrix structures optimize for control and coordination. Agile structures optimize for speed and adaptation. Both require discipline, processes, and governance, but they emphasize different capabilities.

Agile organizations scale this team-based approach through frameworks that reproduce team dynamics across multiple teams. When outcomes become too complex for single teams, organizations create networks of aligned teams rather than management hierarchies. New coordination roles emerge - product managers, tribe leaders, chapter heads, release train engineers - but these aren't traditional "boss" positions with command-and-control authority.

Instead, these roles function as facilitators and coordinators who enable team effectiveness rather than directing team activities. They're accountable for removing obstacles, facilitating alignment, and ensuring teams have the information and resources needed for success. But they don't make decisions for teams or take responsibility for team outcomes.

This distinction matters enormously for modern tech companies. Traditional management roles often become bottlenecks in fast-moving technical environments. When every decision requires management approval, velocity slows to management processing speed. When managers who don't understand implications and trade-offs make decisions, both speed and quality suffer.

Agile organizations push decision-making authority down to the people closest to the challenges, market requirements and customer realities. Teams make independent decisions. They choose priorities, tools and practices. They decide how to organize their work and measure their progress.

This doesn't eliminate the need for strategic guidance, resource allocation, or performance management. But it changes how these functions operate. Strategy becomes a set of outcome-focused objectives rather than detailed activity plans. Resource allocation focuses on team capabilities rather than project budgets. Performance management emphasizes team results rather than individual tasks.

The transformation from matrix to agile requires more than structural changes. It demands a fundamental shift in how leaders think about control, accountability, and value creation. The next challenge becomes defining new roles and responsibilities that support autonomous teams while maintaining organizational coherence.

Organizing Autonomy: The New Role Structure

Instaffo's CEO Christoph Zoeller faced a familiar problem. His talent acquisition company had grown successfully using traditional functional divisions - sales handled client acquisition, customer success managed ongoing relationships; while separate teams handled candidates and business development. The structure worked until it didn't.

The breaking point came when conflicting incentives between sales and customer success created expensive problems. Sales optimized for quick revenue closure while customer success dealt with unrealistic client expectations and unsustainable service commitments. Revenue grew, but so did costs and customer complaints. Zoeller realized they were operationally distant from customers despite being in the customer service business.

His solution? Complete organizational redesign around what he called the "orbit model" - a radical departure from functional silos toward customer-centric teams.

The transformation shows how successful agile organizations balance different people types and capabilities within cohesive team structures. Rather than segregating skills into separate departments, they integrate diverse capabilities into cross-functional units focused on customer outcomes.

Squads: The Foundation of Value Creation

Squads represent the basic unit of work in agile organizations. These teams contain all the profiles and roles necessary to deliver complete value to customers - developers, product owners, quality engineers, user experience designers, and facilitators (often called scrum masters). They operate with full autonomy and responsibility for specific products, features, or customer segments.

The key principle is end-to-end accountability. Squads don't hand off work to other teams for completion. They don't escalate routine decisions to management. They don't split responsibilities across functional boundaries. Instead, they own customer outcomes from conception through delivery and ongoing support.

Instaffo's transformation demonstrates this principle in action. Rather than maintaining separate sales and customer success functions, they created geographic squads that combined both capabilities. Each squad focuses on a specific micro-market defined by location and industry characteristics. Squad members handle both candidate acquisition (B2C) and business development (B2B), creating valuable insights that wouldn't emerge from functional separation.

This integration eliminates the coordination overhead and accountability gaps that plague matrix structures. When someone can't cover their usual responsibilities, other squad members step in seamlessly. The squad maintains full-service capability rather than depending on other departments or escalation processes.

Tribes: Scaling Squad Success

When outcomes become too complex for single squads, organizations create tribes - collections of squads working on related outcomes or serving related customer segments. Tribes typically emerge when customer needs exceed what five to ten people can address effectively, requiring coordination across multiple specialized teams.

The tribe structure maintains squad autonomy while enabling necessary collaboration. Squads within a tribe share common objectives and customer bases, but they retain decision-making authority over their specific areas of responsibility. Tribes don't create management hierarchy; they create alignment and communication channels.

Effective tribes operate more like jazz ensembles than classical orchestras. They have shared themes and rhythms (strategic objectives and operating principles) but allow individual squads to improvise and innovate within that framework. This balance enables coordination and creativity - squads can respond quickly to local opportunities while maintaining connection to broader organizational purposes.

Chapters: Preserving Excellence Across Teams

Chapters address a critical challenge in squad-based organizations: maintaining and advancing professional expertise. While squads focus on specific outcomes, chapters ensure that people with similar roles share knowledge, methods, and professional standards across the organization.

For example, a "front-end development" chapter might include developers from multiple squads who need to align on technical approaches, share new tools and techniques, and maintain consistent code quality standards. A "product management" chapter enables product owners across different squads to share customer insights, coordinate feature roadmaps, and develop better customer research methods. A "Go-To-Market" chapter is a shared agile capability group that ensures products are launched, positioned, sold and grown effectively while staying tightly embedded in autonomous delivery teams.

Chapters prevent the professional isolation that can occur when specialists are distributed across customer-focused teams. They create communities of practice that advance individual capabilities while serving team objectives. This dual focus - professional excellence and team success - ensures that agile organizations don't sacrifice technical quality for delivery speed.

Guilds: Cross-Pollinating Innovation

Guilds operate at an even broader level, bringing together people from multiple tribes around shared interests or emerging capabilities. While chapters focus on specific roles, guilds explore broader topics that span multiple disciplines and teams.

A "web technologies" guild might include front-end developers, back-end engineers, user experience designers, and product managers who want to explore new possibilities in web development. A "machine learning" guild could bring together data scientists, engineers, and product people interested in AI applications.

Guilds serve as innovation incubators and knowledge-sharing platforms. They identify emerging trends, experiment with new approaches, and transfer insights across organizational boundaries. This cross-pollination prevents teams from becoming insular while maintaining their customer focus.

The Delicate Balance of Structure and Freedom

This role architecture might seem complex, but it serves a crucial purpose: enabling autonomy without creating chaos. Squads have freedom to operate independently while chapters maintain professional standards, tribes coordinate related efforts, and guilds spark innovation across boundaries.

The structure also addresses Conway's Law - the principle that organizations design systems that mirror their communication patterns. Traditional hierarchical structures create products with hierarchical user experiences, rigid interfaces, and departmental boundaries that frustrate customers. Agile role architectures create products with seamless user experiences, integrated functionality, and customer-centric design.

The most successful implementations adapt these concepts rather than copying them exactly. Spotify's model, often cited as the definitive example, has evolved significantly since its initial description. Even Spotify has moved beyond their original framework as they've grown and market conditions have changed.

The key insight isn't the specific names or structures - it's the underlying principles. Successful agile organizations create roles that support team autonomy while maintaining organizational coherence. They balance customer focus with professional excellence. They enable innovation while ensuring operational excellence.

But the most challenging transformation isn't structural - it's cultural. The shift from traditional management roles to agile facilitation requires leaders who can enable success rather than direct activities.

The Leadership Paradox: Making Yourself Unnecessary

Martina had built her career on being indispensable. As Director of Product Engineering, she prided herself on knowing every project detail, approving every technical decision, and solving every team conflict. Her direct reports came to her for guidance on everything from architecture choices to personnel issues. She was the hub through which all information flowed.

Then her company started their agile transformation journey.

The consultant's first question stopped her cold: "What would happen if your teams could operate effectively without you for a month?"

Martina's immediate reaction was defensive. "They need my experience and oversight. Without central coordination, we'd have chaos. Quality would suffer. Projects would go off track."

Six months later, Martina discovered something that initially terrified her: her teams performed better when she stopped trying to control everything.

Is there a place for middle management in agile organizations? The uncomfortable truth is - not as traditionally practiced. Most companies lack the courage to fundamentally reposition managers who have climbed hierarchical ladders over years or decades. This reluctance leads to failed transformations that layer agile practices over command-and-control structures.

But there's absolutely a place for management in agile organizations - just not the way it's been done historically.

The Servant Leader Revolution

The agile manager's position fundamentally differs from traditional management. Instead of being the primary decision-maker and performance director, the agile manager becomes a servant leader whose main goal is building trust, creating psychological safety, and removing impediments for teams.

Think of this role as like a scrum master but operating at a higher organizational level. Where scrum masters facilitate individual team effectiveness, agile managers facilitate ecosystem effectiveness across multiple teams and organizational boundaries.

Many organizations describe this as "leader-coach" because both competencies are essential. Agile managers need leadership skills to drive vision and strategic alignment while developing coaching capabilities to ensure individual and collective improvement. They don't just direct people toward goals; they develop people's capability to achieve increasingly ambitious goals.

Living the Values, not just Preaching Them

Agile managers embody the values and principles of agility and their organization's specific culture. This isn't about posting value statements on walls or mentioning them in presentations. It's about demonstrating through daily decisions and interactions what customer obsession, team empowerment, and continuous improvement look like in practice.

When team members observe their manager prioritizing customer needs over internal convenience, taking accountability for failures rather than assigning blame, and investing in long-term capability rather than short-term results, they learn more about organizational values than any training program could teach.

This modeling becomes particularly crucial during difficult periods. When market pressures mount, deadlines approach, or conflicts arise, the agile manager's response sets the tone for how teams navigate challenges. Do they revert to command-and-control patterns under stress? Do they sacrifice long-term team health for short-term deliverables? Or do they maintain agile principles precisely when those principles become most difficult to follow?

The Ambassador Function

Agile managers serve as ambassadors between their tribes or product areas and the broader organization. They translate strategic context into team-relevant objectives. They communicate team innovations and insights to other parts of the organization. They advocate for resources and support that teams need for success.

This ambassador role becomes especially important in large organizations where teams can become isolated from strategic context or where other departments don't understand agile operating principles. The agile manager helps teams understand how their work contributes to larger organizational success while helping the organization understand how to support team effectiveness.

The Ultimate Goal: Making Yourself Unnecessary

Here's the statement that creates significant silence in leadership rooms: **agile managers should strive to make themselves unnecessary**.

This doesn't mean eliminating the position or abandoning teams. It means developing team capabilities to the point where teams can operate autonomously and effectively without constant management intervention. The ultimate question isn't "How can I control and steer this team?" but "What does this team lack to be completely autonomous and efficient?"

Most managers operate in self-preservation mode, protecting their territory, justifying their positions, and maintaining dependencies that prove their value. This behavior optimizes for individual job security rather than organizational effectiveness, team development, or customer outcomes.

Agile managers ask different questions: What obstacles prevent this team from delivering value faster? What skills do team members need to make better decisions independently? What information or authority is missing that forces unnecessary escalation? How can I develop people's capabilities rather than their dependence?

The goal isn't to eliminate management - there will always be needs for leadership, coaching, and organizational facilitation. The goal is reaching toward a state where teams are capable, confident, and empowered to handle increasingly complex challenges without requiring constant oversight.

The Practical Transformation

Martina's transformation illustrates this evolution. Instead of approving every technical decision, she helped her teams develop decision-making frameworks and escalation criteria. Rather than solving every conflict, she taught teams conflict resolution skills and created psychological safety for difficult conversations.

Most importantly, she shifted from being the bottleneck to being the capability multiplier. When teams encountered technical challenges beyond their current expertise, she connected them with resources and mentors rather than solving problems for them. When strategic questions arose, she facilitated discussions that helped teams understand context and make informed choices.

The result? Her teams moved faster, made better decisions, and developed stronger technical capabilities. Martina discovered that enabling others' success felt more rewarding than being the hero who solved every problem.

Agile management represents just one element of successful enterprise agility. The real challenge lies in systematically implementing these principles across entire organizations without losing momentum or reverting to familiar patterns.

Making It Real: From Vision to Velocity

I recently had an eye-opening conversation with Bernd, a senior executive of a leading German car manufacturer. We met at a conference in Italy where he was presenting their agile transformation journey. He is driving agile transformation across different functions within the company including finance where his original background is.

When I asked him about his thoughts on global competition, he stated, "We're not losing to better technology or cheaper production; we are losing to speed," and added, "We're losing to better organizational design." He pointed out that some Chinese car manufacturers are achieving similar results but three times faster. Transforming his organization is not a nice to have but critical for survival.

A successful shift to enterprise agility generally starts with intense focus on improving customer value delivery in small, rapid increments. But the technical aspects - implementing Scrum ceremonies, creating cross-functional teams, or adopting DevOps practices - represent only the visible portion of transformation. The deeper challenge involves addressing human and emotional intelligence aspects that determine whether teams genuinely embrace new ways of working.

Change is inherently difficult, and enterprise agility efforts involve simultaneous changes across organizational structures, operational processes, technology tools, and success metrics. Most people can handle one significant change at a time. Agile transformation asks them to handle multiple interconnected changes while maintaining daily productivity and customer service levels.

Bernd reported that during their transition, some team members left to more traditional parts of the organization or left entirely. Other employees asked to join his team as they wanted to be part of this change and appreciated the new ways of working. There should be no doubt, true organizational re-design towards an agile operating model is challenging and requires empathic and experienced leaders. The rewards are game changing though.

Research from organizations that have completed successful enterprise-wide transformations reveals that agility improvements compound over time. Companies typically see **ten-to-thirty-point increases** in customer satisfaction scores alongside **twenty-to-thirty-nine-point improvements** in employee engagement. These improvements reinforce each other - engaged employees deliver better customer experiences, while satisfied customers provide clearer feedback that enables employee success.

But the path isn't linear. Most organizations experience initial performance dips as people adjust to new working methods, decision-making processes, and collaboration patterns. The transformation requires sustaining commitment through these temporary setbacks while maintaining confidence in long-term benefits.

Creating Shared Purpose that Inspires Action

Every successful enterprise agility transformation begins with developing shared purpose that inspires employees and delights customers. This isn't a marketing exercise or strategic planning session. It's discovering the fundamental reason your organization exists beyond generating profit and articulating that purpose in language that guides daily decisions.

Amazon's "Earth's most customer-centric company" exemplifies effective organizational purpose. It's specific enough to guide decisions - when facing trade-offs, choose the option that better serves customers. It's inspirational enough to motivate effort - people want to contribute to something meaningful. And it's measurable enough to assess progress - customer satisfaction metrics directly reflect purpose achievement.

Your purpose becomes the North Star that enables autonomous decision-making throughout the organization. When teams understand the ultimate outcome they're serving, they can make rapid choices without escalating routine decisions through management hierarchies. Purpose doesn't replace leadership; it enables distributed leadership at every organizational level.

Building Agile Team Culture

Successful agile transformations create team cultures that increase communication within teams while decreasing coordination overhead across groups. This seems counterintuitive - more internal communication usually means more overall communication - but the math works differently in agile structures.

Traditional organizations require extensive cross-functional coordination because work gets handed off between specialized departments. Marketing defines requirements, engineering builds features, quality assurance tests functionality, operations handles deployment, and customer support manages ongoing issues. Each handoff requires coordination meetings, documentation, and alignment processes.

Agile teams internalize these capabilities, dramatically reducing external coordination needs. When teams contain all necessary skills and authority to deliver customer value, they coordinate internally rather than externally. The total communication volume might increase, but the coordination complexity decreases significantly.

Adopting Product Mindset over Project Thinking

One of the most crucial shifts involves moving from project-based thinking to product-based thinking. Projects have defined beginnings, middles, and ends. They optimize for completing predetermined scope within fixed timelines and budgets. Success means finishing what was planned.

Products have ongoing life cycles with evolving customer needs and market conditions. They optimize for creating sustainable customer value over time. Success means continuously improving customer outcomes and business results.

This shift changes how organizations allocate resources, measure success, and make strategic decisions. Instead of funding projects with fixed scope and timelines, organizations fund product teams with ongoing capability to deliver value. Instead of measuring project completion rates, they measure customer satisfaction and business impact.

Expanding Perspectives through Collaborative Discovery

Traditional organizations rely on subject matter experts to define requirements, make technical decisions, and solve complex problems. This expertise-driven approach works well for known problems with established solutions but struggles with novel challenges or rapidly changing conditions.

Agile organizations use collaborative discovery processes that include diverse perspectives from the outset. "Three amigos" meetings bring together business, development, and testing perspectives before work begins rather than after problems emerge. Design thinking sessions include customer voices in solution development. Cross-functional workshops generate options that no single discipline would discover independently.

These collaborative approaches take more time initially but save enormous amounts of rework, miscommunication, and failed solutions. They also develop organizational learning capabilities that enable faster response to future challenges.

Encouraging Cross-Role Learning and Development

Enterprise agility requires people who can apply knowledge across broad ranges of situations while maintaining deep expertise in specific areas. This T-shaped skill profile - broad knowledge, deep specialization - enables the flexibility that agile teams need to respond to changing priorities and unexpected challenges.

Organizations support this development by encouraging cross-role training, rotating assignments, and collaborative problem-solving. Developers learn user experience principles. Product managers understand technical constraints. Designers appreciate business requirements. Everyone develops customer empathy.

This cross-training doesn't eliminate specialization - teams still need deep functional expertise, strong design capabilities, and sharp business acumen. But it creates shared understanding that enables better collaboration and faster adaptation.

Creating Value-Driven Development Workflows

The final element involves establishing business development workflows that allow teams to create customer value in small increments rather than large, infrequent releases.

Value-driven workflows change the rhythm of work from quarterly planning cycles and annual product releases to weekly delivery cycles and continuous improvement processes. Teams ship small improvements frequently rather than major updates occasionally. They collect customer feedback rapidly and incorporate insights into ongoing improvement rather than waiting for the next planning cycle. But don't stop at development; the same applies for sales, marketing finance, customer success, and IT. They are all an integral part of what makes your customers happy and therefore your company successful.

Seven Steps to Start Your Enterprise Agility Journey

Transform your organization's agility with these specific, actionable steps:

Document Your Current State

Before changing anything, map your organization's current agility level using assessment frameworks covering strategy, structure, process, people, and technology. Identify the three biggest barriers preventing faster customer value delivery. Document decision-making speed for routine and complex choices.

Define Future State using your North Star

Define your desired organizational state. Start with your North Star vision and how you deliver the promised value to your customers. Then work backwards through your organization and what functions and processes are touched to deliver that promise. Map out what an ideal process flow would look like from a customer point of view.

Build a Team of Champions

Build a team of champions that are open to drive the agile transformation approach. You will need champions in different functional areas that are willing to support you and open to act in the unknown. They should have a high level of empathy, be good communicators and able to inspire people.

Involve an Agile Transformation Expert

Find an experienced expert on agile transformation and explain your above discovered current state and desired future state. Work out a staged plan and discuss time line, risk, and risk mitigation strategies. I would recommend a SAFe certified profession or a consulting company experienced with SAFe. Scaled Agile is a great starting point but it is important to develop your own variation that fits best for your unique business.

Work out a Communication Plan

Communication will be a key element of your agile transformation process. It is important that every part of your organization understands your North Star vision and understands where the company is heading. Change is scary for many people so the better your communication the less distraction. Develop your messaging before starting the transformation to ensure you are not in a rush to communicate.

Pick Your First Value Stream

Choose one customer journey or business area for initial transformation. Select something important enough to matter but contained enough to manage. Form a cross-functional team with end-to-end accountability for customer outcomes in this area.

Build Your Learning and Adaptation System

Establish weekly retrospectives to capture what's working and what's not. Set up monthly reviews to assess customer impact and team health. Design quarterly alignment sessions to ensure your transformation stays connected to overall business strategy.

Enterprise agility isn't a destination - it's a capability that enables sustainable competitive advantage in dynamic markets. The organizations that develop this capability fastest will define the future of your industry. The question isn't whether to begin this transformation but how quickly you can build momentum toward the adaptive, customer-obsessed organization your market demands.

TEMPLATES

08

CHAPTER

Projects versus Products & Outputs versus Outcomes

Next to an agile organization model another element for efficiency and effectiveness moving from a project and output based operating model to a product and outcome based operating model. In short, projects have a defined start and end date with a fixed scope and funding. Products are ongoing with continuous funding. Outputs are finished tasks and typically measure by the number of tasks completed or elements delivered. Outcomes are desired results typically measure by the value they are generating.

Take my conversation with Bernd in the previous chapter.

When he stated "Most people think it's all about cheaper production costs. The reality is, some of the newer competitors are developing their next generation cars at three times the speed of us. This is why moving to an agile product operating model is so essential for us to stay in the game." This hit me because I'd just experienced something similar a few months earlier. We had announced our latest product release internally and were proud of the new AI capabilities we'd developed. These new features would let users ask for data and status updates in plain English.

Then one of our sales managers said: "That's really great, but I just saw a competitor's presentation that blew me out of the water. They didn't just implement simple AI functionalities but were able to automate their system functionalities in natural language. And this wasn't a prototype - it was their main platform that was available to customers already."

"But the project was delivered on time and within budget," protested our Chief Revenue Officer, a sharp sales executive who'd joined us from a traditional software company. "The product managers hit every milestone we set for them."

That's when I realized we had a fundamental problem - one that would ultimately cost us not just millions in wasted resources but precious market opportunities that our competitors would seize while we stumbled in the dark.

You see, our CRO, despite his impressive track record in sales and marketing, fundamentally misunderstood what product management truly involves. In his world, product managers were simply glorified project managers tasked with delivering predetermined features according to rigid timelines. He measured success by adherence to plans rather than outcomes achieved. Under his leadership, our product teams had become feature factories, churning out functionality without understanding whether it solved real customer problems or created genuine value.

This experience taught me a harsh but invaluable lesson: having brilliant individual contributors means nothing if your operating model doesn't know how to harness their potential. We had talented engineers, creative designers, and customer-focused product managers, but we'd organized them in a way that virtually guaranteed mediocrity. Instead of empowering these teams to solve customer problems and drive business outcomes, we'd reduced them to order-takers executing a predetermined list of features.

The cost was unbelievable. Not just the immediate financial impact of failed initiatives but the opportunity cost of what we could have achieved. While we were busy checking boxes on project plans, nimble competitors were rapidly iterating, learning from customers, and building products that moved the needle for their businesses. They understood something we didn't: in today's technology-driven landscape, your operating model isn't just important - it's your competitive advantage.

As technology becomes the backbone of virtually every industry, every company is becoming a software company whether they realize it or not. But here's what most leaders miss: if you want to compete like a software company, you can't just adopt the tools and technologies - you need to fundamentally rethink how you operate. You need to launch features faster while maintaining quality. You need to build world-class user experiences that delight customers. You need to free up your development teams to focus on work that creates real business impact rather than busy work that merely gives the illusion of progress.

The organizations that master this transformation don't just survive the digital revolution - they lead it. They're the companies that consistently build innovative products that produce meaningful outcomes for customers and shareholders. They move with the speed and agility that today's markets demand while maintaining the strategic focus that drives long-term success.

This transformation hinges on understanding and implementing the **Product Operating Model** - a fundamentally different approach to how cross-functional teams from business, product, engineering, and operations work together to create and deliver solutions. Unlike traditional project-based approaches that focus on completing tasks and hitting deadlines, the product operating model empowers autonomous teams to solve problems and deliver outcomes.

What Is an Operating Model, really?

Think of your organization as a complex machine designed to create value. Every component - from individual roles to decision-making processes to performance metrics - must work in harmony to achieve your strategic objectives. An operating model is essentially the blueprint that describes how all these pieces fit together to deliver that value consistently and efficiently.

The Agile Product Operating Model takes this concept and applies it specifically to how organizations develop and deliver products in our rapidly evolving digital landscape. It's a comprehensive framework that bridges modern product management principles with agile methodologies, creating a foundation that enables teams to respond quickly to change while maintaining focus on meaningful outcomes.

What makes this approach fundamentally different from traditional models is its foundation in what we call the "product mindset." Instead of organizing around temporary projects with predetermined deliverables, the product operating model aligns the entire organization around products - those vehicles through which you invest, manage, and deliver value to customers.

Consider how most organizations currently operate. They break down work into a series of projects, each with its own timeline, budget, and success criteria. Teams focus on delivering against predefined milestones, and success is measured by whether they hit those targets on schedule. The problem with this approach isn't that projects are inherently bad - it's that the project mindset can become restrictive, reducing your team's ability to be flexible and adapt when they discover better ways to solve customer problems.

A well-defined operating model serves as the crucial bridge between your strategic vision and your daily operations. It's the "what" that connects the "why" of your strategy with the "how" of your processes. More importantly, it creates the essential alignment within your organization needed to develop products that deliver genuine value to customers rather than just checking boxes on a project plan.

When we examine organizations that consistently innovate and outperform their competitors, we find they share certain characteristics in their operating models. They've moved beyond the traditional command-and-control structures that slow decision-making and stifle creativity. Instead, they've created environments where cross-functional teams can work autonomously while remaining aligned with broader business objectives.

Project Mindset vs. Product Mindset: The Great Divide

Imagine two software teams tasked with improving customer retention.

The first operates under a traditional project mindset. Leadership has identified a specific set of features they believe will solve the problem - perhaps a loyalty program, enhanced user onboarding, and improved customer support workflows. The team receives detailed requirements, estimates the work, and creates a project plan with milestones spread across six months. Success is measured by delivering these features on time and within budget.

The second team operates with a product mindset. They receive the same challenge - improve customer retention - but instead of predetermined solutions, they're given context about why this matters to the business and what success looks like. They begin by deeply understanding the current customer experience, analyzing data to identify where customers are struggling, and conducting interviews to uncover unmet needs. They might discover that the real retention challenge isn't about loyalty programs at all but about customers not realizing the full value of features they're already paying for.

This fundamental difference in approach explains why organizations with high product operating model maturity achieve **60% higher returns to shareholders** and **16% higher operating margins** compared to their project-focused counterparts. The product-minded team has the flexibility to solve the actual problem rather than building predetermined solutions that may miss the mark entirely.

The project mindset isn't inherently wrong - it emerged from industries where requirements were stable and solutions were predictable. When you're building a bridge or manufacturing a physical product, detailed upfront planning makes sense because changes become exponentially more expensive as you progress. But software and digital products operate under different rules. The cost of change remains relatively low throughout the development process, and customer needs evolve rapidly based on market conditions, competitive pressures, and their own learning.

Here's what the mindset shift really means in practice:

01	Projects focus on outputs - did we deliver what we planned?
02	Products focus on outcomes - did we solve the problem and create value?
03	Projects measure success by adherence to plans
04	Products measure success by customer satisfaction and business impact
05	Projects end when the deliverables are complete
06	Products evolve continuously based on learning and changing needs

This doesn't mean you'll never have projects within a product operating model. Sometimes you'll face cross-product initiatives like compliance requirements, security upgrades, or platform migrations that require project-style coordination. The key difference is that product leadership maintains the authority to balance these project needs against ongoing product priorities, ensuring that cross-cutting work gets integrated thoughtfully rather than derailing product momentum.

Creating this clarity around products and their boundaries becomes the first critical step in adopting the product operating model. You'll need to examine the services your organization provides - external and internal - and group them into coherent products with clear ownership, defined users, and measurable outcomes. Don't expect to get this perfect immediately. Treat it as an inspection and adaptation opportunity, making boundaries transparent and creating clear decision-making authority.

The transformation from project to product thinking represents one of the most significant organizational shifts you can make, and it's often the most challenging because it requires people to fundamentally change how they think about work, success, and value creation.

The Five Core Principles

As Charles Darwin observed, "It is not the strongest of the species that survive, nor the most intelligent, but the one most responsive to change." This insight captures the essence of why the Agile Product Operating Model has become essential for modern organizations. It's not enough to have brilliant people or deep resources - you need an operating model that enables rapid adaptation while maintaining strategic focus.

The framework operates on five foundational principles that guide decision-making and shape organizational behavior:

Principles Over Process

Rigid processes often become obstacles to innovation. Instead of mandating specific procedures, successful organizations establish clear principles that guide teams in making appropriate decisions within their specific contexts.

When Spotify's machine learning engineers saw potential in creating personalized playlists, they didn't need to navigate complex approval processes - they had clear principles about experimentation and customer value that enabled them to move forward quickly.

Trust Over Control

This fundamentally changes how leadership operates. Rather than micromanaging team activities, leaders focus on providing clear objectives and constraints, then trust empowered teams to find the best solutions. This shift requires significant courage from executives accustomed to detailed oversight, but it's essential for achieving the speed and innovation that markets demand.

Innovation Over Predictability

Traditional organizations often prioritize predictable outcomes over breakthrough innovations, leading to incremental improvements that competitors can easily match. The product operating model inverts this priority, accepting that meaningful innovation requires accepting uncertainty and the possibility of failure.

Learning Over Failure

Instead of punishing failures, the model encourages rapid learning through small, controlled experiments that provide valuable insights at minimal cost. This approach allows teams to discover what works without betting the company on untested assumptions.

Outcomes Over Output

Teams focus on solving problems and creating value rather than just finishing tasks. Success gets measured by customer satisfaction and business impact rather than adherence to completion schedules.

The Architecture of Success

Each product operating under this framework requires specific architectural components that work together to enable agile response to market conditions:

Business Roadmap

Your business roadmap must clearly connect product strategies to broader business objectives, ensuring product teams understand how their work contributes to organizational success. This isn't about creating detailed long-term plans - it's about establishing clear direction while maintaining flexibility to adjust based on learning.

Technology Roadmap

This describes how technical capabilities will evolve to support business goals. It becomes crucial for ensuring that short-term product decisions don't create long-term technical debt that constrains future innovation. The most successful organizations treat their technology architecture as a product itself, continuously investing in capabilities that enable faster delivery and better customer experiences.

Operational Stability

This provides the foundation that allows teams to move quickly without breaking critical systems. This includes defining service levels that create transparency about what customers can expect, establishing monitoring and alerting systems that catch problems before they impact users, and building recovery processes that minimize the impact of inevitable failures.

Governance and Flow

These processes determine how changes are managed and controlled without slowing innovation. This represents one of the most delicate balances in the operating model - providing enough oversight to ensure quality and compliance while avoiding bureaucracy that stifles creativity and speed.

Total Cost of Value

Understanding this becomes essential for making informed investment decisions. This goes beyond traditional cost accounting to include opportunity costs, technical debt, and the long-term impact of today's decisions on future capabilities. Organizations that master this analysis can make better trade-offs between short-term delivery and long-term sustainability.

Three Dimensions of Transformation

What does it actually look like when teams operate within this model? The transformation becomes visible across three fundamental dimensions that distinguish high-performing product organizations from their traditional counterparts.

1. How Products Get Built

Organizations operating in the product model abandon the traditional approach of large, infrequent releases in favor of small, frequent, and reliable deployments. Most teams release new capabilities at least every two weeks, though the most mature organizations deploy continuously throughout the day. This isn't just about speed - it's about fundamentally changing the relationship between development and learning.

When Spotify was developing their game-changing Discover Weekly feature, they didn't spend months building a complete solution before testing it with users. Instead, they started with a live-data prototype that they quietly rolled out to employees, then gradually expanded to larger user groups as they validated their assumptions. Each small release provided immediate feedback that informed the next iteration, allowing them to refine the experience based on actual user behavior rather than hypothetical requirements.

This approach enables organizations to respond quickly to customer needs, often addressing problems before customers even realize they exist. It allows teams to prove that new capabilities deliver necessary value rather than hoping they will. Most importantly, it reduces the risk inherent in large releases by making problems smaller and easier to fix.

2. How Problems Get Solved

Instead of receiving predetermined feature lists to implement, product teams working in this model receive problems to solve and outcomes to achieve. This fundamental shift empowers the people closest to the technology and users - engineers, product managers, and designers - to determine the best solutions for addressing assigned challenges.

Consider Amazon's approach to developing Prime. Rather than starting with a predetermined solution, teams received the challenge of improving customer convenience through better shipping experiences. This problem-focused approach led to a series of experiments: Super Saver Shipping, faster shipping options, annual fees for free shipping, and ultimately the revolutionary subscription model that transformed retail forever. Had teams been given specific features to build instead of problems to solve, Amazon Prime as we know it today might never have emerged.

Teams empowered to solve problems focus on creating solutions that are valuable to customers, usable by end users, feasible with available technology and skills, and viable within business constraints. This framework ensures that innovation serves both customer needs and business objectives rather than pursuing clever technical solutions that lack market relevance.

3. How Organizations Decide Which Problems to Solve

In the product operating model, leaders in product management, technology, and design take responsibility for strategic decisions about problem prioritization. They work with stakeholders to drive necessary organizational changes by creating customer-centric product visions and insight-driven product strategies.

This represents a fundamental shift from traditional approaches where product priorities emerge from internal politics, loudest stakeholders, or historical precedent. Instead, product leaders use data, customer research, and market analysis to identify the most critical problems that need solving to achieve business objectives and progress toward product vision.

At Amazon, this strategic approach manifests in their famous "six-pagers" - written narratives that provide evidence and reasoning behind proposed product work. These documents get intensely debated, ensuring resource allocation decisions are based on rigorous analysis rather than intuition or organizational politics. The result is clearer focus, better alignment, and more effective use of limited development resources.

The power of these three dimensions working together creates a compounding effect that explains why organizations successfully operating in the product model consistently outperform their traditional counterparts. They build faster, solve better problems, and focus their efforts on the initiatives most likely to drive meaningful business results.

The Five Elements That Make It Work

The product operating model encompasses five interconnected elements that reinforce each other:

01 **People and Organization**

This defines responsibilities, roles, and how teams are structured to maximize effectiveness. Cross-functional, durable teams receive empowerment to solve problems for customers and create value for the business. These teams typically include product managers, designers, and engineers working together on shared objectives rather than operating as separate functional silos.

02 **Measures and Incentives**

This establishes key performance indicators and how success is communicated throughout the organization. Instead of measuring outputs like features shipped or story points completed, the focus shifts to outcomes like customer satisfaction, business impact, and learning velocity.

03 **Agile Processes**

This describes how people work together and what information they need to deliver value efficiently. This includes product discovery processes for rapidly determining the best solutions to assigned problems and product delivery focused on building, testing, and deploying quality solutions.

04 **Governance Structures**

This determines who makes decisions and what oversight mechanisms ensure quality and alignment. Rather than command-and-control structures, governance becomes about providing clear objectives and constraints while trusting teams to find optimal solutions.

05 **Culture and Behavior**

This reflects the values, beliefs, and attitudes that influence how work gets done. The culture embraces experimentation, learning from failure, customer obsession, and continuous improvement.

What's crucial to understand is you can't implement only one or two of these elements and expect to see results. They work as an integrated system. Your processes require people to be organized in specific ways. Your governance structure affects your culture. Your tools and technology must support everything else. The product mindset and agile principles provide the constraints that unify these elements into a coherent operating model that drives consistent results.

Your Next Steps

The journey toward implementing a product operating model begins with honest assessment and deliberate action. Here are five specific steps you can take immediately to begin this transformation:

Audit Your Current Initiatives

Examine the initiatives your organization is working on and group them into coherent products with clear ownership, defined contributors, and measurable outcomes. Don't aim for perfection - focus on creating transparency and clear decision-making authority.

Identify One Team Ready for Empowerment

Choose a cross-functional team working on a meaningful initiative and give them outcome-based objectives instead of output-based requirements. Support them with the autonomy and resources needed to experiment and learn.

Establish Rapid Feedback Mechanisms

Invest in the instrumentation, monitoring, and deployment infrastructure that enables small, frequent iterations and real-time learning about what's working and what isn't.

Align Leadership on Product Principles

Work with your executive team to establish clear principles that will guide decision-making as you transform. Focus especially on principles over process and trust over control.

Create Your Transformation Roadmap

Treat your operating model transformation as a product itself, with clear vision, strategy, and success metrics. Plan your evolution in quarterly cycles that allow for meaningful progress while maintaining flexibility to adapt based on learning.

TEMPLATES

The companies that will thrive in the next decade won't be the ones with the most resources or the smartest individuals - they'll be the ones that build operating models capable of continuous adaptation and innovation.

Organizations that successfully implement this model report dramatic improvements in their ability to respond to market changes, reduce time to market, and increase customer satisfaction. They discover that empowering teams with clear objectives and appropriate autonomy doesn't create chaos - it unleashes innovation and drives business results that traditional approaches simply can't match.

The transformation to the product operating model represents one of the most significant competitive advantages available to modern organizations. Companies that master this approach don't merely survive digital transformation - they lead their industries by consistently delivering innovations that create value for customers and drive business growth.

But understanding the concepts isn't enough. Implementation requires systematic effort, leadership commitment, and willingness to evolve your approach based on learning and experience. The organizations that succeed treat the transformation itself as a product, applying the same principles of experimentation, measurement, and continuous improvement to their operating model they apply to their customer-facing products.

09

CHAPTER

Making Decisions Based on What Works

I remember Amina, a brilliant CTO of a fintech company, staring at her quarterly metrics dashboard late one evening. Revenue was up 18%, customer acquisition costs had dropped by 12%, and team velocity showed consistent improvement. By every traditional measure, her organization was crushing it. Yet something felt off - a persistent unease that all these glowing numbers might be telling her everything except what mattered.

Three months earlier, Amina had made what seemed like a data-driven decision to prioritize feature development over infrastructure improvements. The metrics supported this choice: user requests for new features outweighed infrastructure complaints by a ratio of 7:1. Her team delivered those features on schedule, hitting every milestone. But now, as customer support tickets multiplied and system outages became more frequent, Amina realized she'd been measuring the wrong things entirely.

This scenario plays out in software companies across the globe every day. We're drowning in data yet starving for genuine insight. We track everything that's easy to measure while the most critical indicators of long-term success remain invisible to our dashboards. The irony is profound: in an industry built on precision and logic, we often make decisions based on intuition disguised as analysis.

Here's the uncomfortable truth that most executives won't admit - having more data doesn't automatically lead to better decisions. In fact, it can create a dangerous illusion of certainty that masks fundamental blind spots. Traditional metrics often measure activity rather than value, outputs rather than outcomes, and present performance rather than future potential.

What Amina needed - what every technology leader needs - is a framework that cuts through the noise of vanity metrics to focus on what drives sustainable value. She needed to embrace what leading organizations have discovered: the power of evidence-based management.

This isn't about collecting more data or creating prettier dashboards. It's about fundamentally shifting how we think about measurement itself. Instead of asking, "How much did we do?" we learn to ask, "How much value did we create?" Instead of celebrating busy work, we focus on meaningful progress. Instead of making decisions based on assumptions dressed up as insights, we create systems that generate real evidence about what works and what doesn't.

Organizations that master this approach don't just outperform their competitors - they operate in an entirely different league. They make decisions with clarity while others guess. They adapt quickly while others struggle with change. They create sustained value while others chase quarterly numbers that ultimately lead nowhere.

The Foundation: What Evidence Really Means

The morning after her late-night realization, Amina did something that surprised her team. Instead of calling another strategy meeting or commissioning another analysis, she gathered her leadership team and asked a simple question: "What evidence do we have that our customers are actually better off because of what we built last quarter?"

The silence that followed wasn't due to lack of preparation - it revealed something far more significant. Despite having more performance data than ever before, they couldn't clearly articulate how their efforts had meaningfully improved their customers' lives. They had outputs in abundance but struggled to identify genuine outcomes.

This moment marked Amina's first encounter with a crucial distinction that transforms how successful leaders think about measurement. Evidence-based management isn't another methodology to implement - it's a lens that reveals whether your organization is creating real value or simply staying busy.

Think about how most software organizations operate: they set goals based on historical performance, measure progress through activity metrics, and celebrate hitting targets that may have little connection to actual value creation. It's like navigating with a compass that points toward magnetic north when you need to reach true north.

Evidence-based management provides that true north by focusing on a fundamental principle: organizations exist to achieve something meaningful that they, uniquely, can accomplish. This purpose gets expressed through vision statements that articulate the change they want to create in the world, mission statements that explain why they're uniquely capable of achieving that vision, and goals that create concrete progress toward both.

But here's where most organizations stumble. They create lofty mission and vision statements that sound inspiring in boardrooms but fail to translate into daily decision-making. Without specific, measurable goals connected to genuine value creation, these statements remain empty aspirations. Teams end up optimizing for metrics that feel important but don't move the organization toward its deeper purpose.

The genius of evidence-based management lies in its systematic approach to closing this gap. It creates a framework that helps organizations form more effective goals at three distinct levels:

STRATEGIC GOALS

These represent the important things an organization needs to achieve to realize its mission and vision. They're inherently ambitious and far-reaching, with many uncertainties along the journey. They're aspirational by design - the kind of bold objectives that require learning because the path to achieving them isn't entirely clear from the outset.

INTERMEDIATE GOALS

These serve as practical targets that indicate the organization is making progress toward its strategic goals. While still somewhat uncertain, the path to achieving these goals is more visible and manageable. They function as waypoints that help organizations know they're heading in the right direction while remaining flexible about exactly how they'll reach their ultimate destination.

IMMEDIATE TACTICAL GOALS

These provide the current focus for improvement efforts. They're concrete, near-term objectives that teams can work toward with clarity and confidence. They're specific enough to guide daily decisions yet flexible enough to evolve based on what the organization learns through experimentation.

The relationship between these three levels creates a powerful dynamic. Teams work toward immediate tactical goals through specific experiments designed to test ideas about improvement. They measure the results of these experiments to evaluate progress toward their goals and determine next steps. This approach - forming hypotheses, running experiments, checking results, and adapting based on learning - transforms abstract strategic thinking into concrete progress.

Turning Assumptions into Experiments

Three weeks into her evidence-based transformation, Amina faced her first real test. A major client had requested a feature that would require significant development resources. Under her old approach, she would have analyzed market research, projected ROI, and made a decision based on best available information. But now she recognized something crucial: beliefs about value are merely assumptions until customers validate them.

Instead of committing fully to the feature, Amina's team designed an experiment. They created a minimum viable version that addressed the core need, released it to a small group of customers, and measured not just usage but actual impact on customer success. What they discovered challenged everything they thought they knew about their market.

The experiment revealed that customers used the feature differently than expected, valued different aspects than anticipated, and experienced benefits that hadn't appeared in any requirements document. More importantly, the experiment cost 15% of what full development would have required while generating 80% of the value customers wanted.

This experience illustrates the heart of evidence-based management: **every feature, every requirement, every strategic initiative represents a hypothesis about value**. Rather than treating these hypotheses as facts, successful organizations design experiments to test them systematically.

The Experiment Loop

The experiment loop that guides this process follows a simple pattern:

1. **Form hypotheses** about improvements they believe will move them toward their goals
2. **Design and run experiments** to test these hypotheses, gathering data about actual results rather than assumed outcomes
3. **Inspect results** against their expectations, learning what worked, what didn't, and why
4. **Adapt their approach** based on this learning, which may include adjusting their goals, refining their methods, or forming new hypotheses to test

This loop transforms the traditional relationship between planning and execution. Instead of creating elaborate plans based on assumptions, teams plan experiments based on hypotheses. Instead of measuring success by how well they executed the plan, they measure success by how much they learned and how effectively they adapted.

The power of this approach becomes clear when you consider how most software projects unfold. Requirements change. Market conditions shift. Customer needs evolve. Technology constraints emerge. Traditional project management treats these changes as problems to be minimized. Evidence-based thinking treats them as information to be leveraged.

Quality Hypotheses Matter

Strong hypotheses are specific, testable, and connected to measurable outcomes. They follow a simple pattern: **"We believe that [specific action] will lead to [specific outcome] as measured by [specific indicators]."**

Strong hypotheses also acknowledge uncertainty explicitly. They're not predictions disguised as experiments - they're genuine questions about what will happen under specific conditions. This mindset shift, from trying to prove we're right to trying to learn what's true, fundamentally changes how organizations approach innovation and improvement.

The Four Key Value Areas

Amina's breakthrough moment came when she realized that her company's impressive-looking metrics were creating a dangerous blind spot. They were measuring everything except whether customers were genuinely better off. Revenue per customer was rising, but customer satisfaction surveys revealed growing frustration. Development velocity was accelerating, but technical debt was accumulating faster than anyone realized.

She needed a more balanced approach - one that could illuminate different aspects of value creation simultaneously. This is where evidence-based management's four key value areas proved transformational, providing complementary lenses that together create a complete picture of organizational performance.

Current Value

This examines the value your organization delivers to customers and stakeholders right now. It focuses exclusively on present reality, not future potential. The fundamental questions center on happiness and satisfaction: How happy are your customers today, and is that happiness improving or declining? How satisfied are your employees, and what trends are emerging? How pleased are your investors and stakeholders with current results?

This dimension often reveals uncomfortable truths. Organizations can show impressive growth metrics while customer satisfaction erodes. They can celebrate team productivity while employee engagement plummets. They can achieve short-term financial targets while undermining long-term stakeholder confidence.

Amina discovered this firsthand when customer interviews revealed that while users appreciated new features, they were increasingly frustrated with system reliability. The company's focus on feature velocity had come at the expense of stability - a trade-off that threatened future growth even as it drove current metrics.

Unrealized Value

This examines the potential future value you could capture if you better met the needs of existing and potential customers. This dimension examines the gap between current customer experience and desired customer experience.

Unrealized value asks provocative questions: What additional value could we create in our current market or adjacent markets? Is it worth the effort and risk to pursue these opportunities? Should we invest more heavily to capture this potential, or are we better served focusing elsewhere?

For Amina's company, exploring unrealized value revealed significant opportunities in enterprise security features that current customers wanted but weren't available. More intriguingly, it showed potential for expanding into adjacent markets where their core technology could solve different but related problems.

The relationship between current value and unrealized value creates strategic clarity. Products with low current value but high unrealized value may warrant significant investment despite poor current performance. Conversely, products with high current value but low unrealized value may not justify continued major investment.

Ability to Innovate

This measures how effectively your organization delivers new capabilities and innovative solutions. It examines what prevents you from delivering new value and what prevents customers from benefiting from your innovations. This dimension reveals whether your organization is building the capabilities needed for sustained success.

Common barriers to innovation include technical debt that consumes development resources, poor product quality that requires constant fixes, organizational inefficiencies that slow decision-making, and inability to attract and retain talented team members. Each of these factors reduces the organization's capacity to create new value.

Amina's team discovered that their ability to innovate was being undermined by several factors they hadn't been measuring. Multiple product versions required ongoing maintenance. Poor automated testing meant manual effort for every release. Unclear product requirements led to rework and delays. These hidden costs were consuming nearly 40% of their development capacity.

Time-to-Market

This measures how quickly the organization can deliver new value and learn from customer feedback. This isn't just about speed - it's about the organization's ability to respond to change, test new ideas, and adapt based on results.

Organizations with poor time-to-market struggle to capitalize on opportunities, respond to competitive threats, or adjust to changing customer needs. They may have great ideas and strong capabilities, but their inability to act quickly undermines their effectiveness in dynamic markets.

The Power of Balance

The four key value areas work together to create a balanced perspective on organizational performance. Current value and unrealized value focus on market outcomes - the value customers experience. Ability to innovate and time-to-market focus on organizational capabilities - the organization's capacity to deliver that value effectively.

Organizations that excel in all four areas create sustainable competitive advantages. They deliver strong current results while building capabilities for future success. They understand their market position while developing the agility to adapt as conditions change.

The beauty of this framework lies in its ability to reveal hidden relationships and trade-offs. Investments that improve time-to-market may temporarily reduce current value but increase long-term unrealized value. Efforts to enhance ability to innovate may require short-term resource allocation that affects immediate metrics but builds future capabilities.

Building Learning Capabilities

Six months after beginning her evidence-based transformation, Amina reflected on the profound changes at her organization. The metrics dashboard still displayed numbers, but now those numbers told a coherent story about value creation rather than just activity. More importantly, her organization had developed capabilities that went far beyond better measurement - they had become a learning organization in the truest sense.

The transformation hadn't been about implementing new tools or processes. It had required fundamental shifts in how they approached goals, decisions, and improvement. These shifts represented capabilities that would serve them regardless of future challenges or opportunities.

Better Goal Formation

Evidence-based organizations excel at forming goals that matter. Instead of setting targets based on historical performance or competitive benchmarking, they align strategic goals directly with their mission and vision while expressing them in terms of customer outcomes and satisfaction gaps.

Think about how this differs from typical goal-setting approaches. Most organizations create goals by asking, "How can we do better than last year?" or "How can we match our competitors?" Evidence-based organizations ask, "What customer outcomes would indicate we're successfully fulfilling our mission?" This shift in questioning leads to fundamentally different - and more meaningful - objectives.

Systematic Experimentation

Evidence-based organizations excel at hypothesis formation and experimentation. Every initiative begins with explicit hypotheses about how specific actions will create specific value. These hypotheses are testable, measurable, and connected to organizational goals.

This approach transforms how teams think about their work. Instead of implementing solutions, they test hypotheses. Instead of assuming value, they design experiments to validate or disprove their assumptions. Instead of defending decisions, they evaluate results objectively and adapt accordingly.

Meaningful Measurement

The measurement capabilities of evidence-based organizations extend far beyond traditional metrics. They distinguish between inputs, activities, outputs, outcomes, and impacts - focusing primarily on outcomes that represent genuine customer value. They understand that measuring activities and outputs is easy while measuring outcomes requires more sophisticated thinking, but they invest in this capability because it drives better decisions.

Amina's team learned to measure customer happiness directly through outcome-focused indicators rather than inferring it from usage statistics. They tracked employee engagement through meaningful work satisfaction rather than only productivity metrics. They evaluated investor value through sustainable capability building rather than just quarterly financial performance.

Continuous Adaptation

Evidence-based organizations develop superior adaptation capabilities. They inspect results systematically, comparing actual outcomes against expected results. When experiments succeed, they scale successful approaches. When experiments fail, they extract learning and design better experiments.

This adaptation process extends to goals themselves. Evidence-based organizations regularly evaluate whether their immediate tactical goals remain appropriate, whether their intermediate goals still point toward strategic objectives and whether their strategic goals reflect current understanding of their mission and market reality.

The combination of these capabilities creates organizational agility that goes beyond operational efficiency. Evidence-based organizations can navigate uncertainty because they've built systems for continuous learning and adaptation. They can respond to unexpected challenges because their decision-making processes emphasize evidence over assumptions.

Getting Started: Your Evidence-Based Journey

The question that inevitably arises is how to begin this transformation in your organization. Amina's experience offers a practical roadmap, but the specific path depends on your current situation, organizational culture, and strategic priorities. The key is starting with small, manageable changes that demonstrate value while building capabilities for more comprehensive implementation.

Examine Your Goals

Begin by examining your current goal-setting process. Most organizations can immediately improve by ensuring their strategic goals connect clearly to customer outcomes rather than internal metrics. Ask yourself: If we achieved our current strategic goals perfectly, would our customers and stakeholders be meaningfully better off? If the answer isn't obviously yes, your goals may be more about internal optimization than value creation.

Turn One Initiative into an Experiment

Identify one significant initiative currently underway in your organization. Transform this initiative into an experiment by making explicit the hypothesis it represents. What specific customer outcome do you expect this initiative to create? How will you measure whether that outcome materializes? What would constitute success, and what would indicate the need to adapt your approach?

This single transformation - from initiative to experiment - often reveals gaps in thinking that have been invisible. Teams may discover they're not clear about expected outcomes, haven't defined success criteria, or lack ways to measure what they're trying to achieve.

Pick One Value Area to Measure

Start measuring one key value area systematically. Choose the area where you currently have the least visibility or where improvement would create the most significant impact. If you're not clear about customer satisfaction, focus on current value. If you're unsure about market opportunities, examine unrealized value. If development seems slow or inefficient, investigate time-to-market or ability to innovate.

The key is selecting measures that directly indicate value creation rather than activity completion. For current value, this might mean customer satisfaction scores, product usage patterns that indicate success, or employee engagement metrics that predict retention. For unrealized value, consider customer feedback about unmet needs, market research about adjacent opportunities, or analysis of competitor advantages.

Create Learning Cycles

Establish regular inspection and adaptation cycles. Schedule monthly or quarterly reviews that examine evidence from your experiments, evaluate progress toward goals, and adjust approaches based on learning. These reviews should focus on what the evidence reveals rather than whether teams hit their targets.

Build Psychological Safety

Create psychological safety for experimentation and learning. Teams must feel comfortable running experiments that might fail, reporting results honestly, and adapting approaches based on evidence. This requires leadership behavior that celebrates learning over success and treats unexpected results as valuable information rather than failures.

For Amina, this meant fundamentally changing how she led. Instead of being the person with answers, she became the person asking better questions. Instead of driving consensus around her vision, she helped her team form hypotheses they could test together. Instead of protecting her team from uncertainty, she helped them develop capabilities for navigating uncertainty successfully.

Your Leadership Opportunity

As leaders in software and technology organizations, you face decisions every day that could dramatically impact your company's future. The question isn't whether you have enough data - you're drowning in it. The question is whether you generate the right evidence to guide decisions that matter.

The leaders who thrive in the coming decade won't be those who perfect predictive planning or optimize existing processes. They'll be those who build organizations capable of learning faster, adapting quicker, and creating value more consistently than their competitors.

Evidence-based management provides the framework for developing these crucial capabilities.

Think about the decisions you'll face in the next quarter. Product development priorities. Resource allocation choices. Market expansion opportunities. Technology investment decisions. Each represents a hypothesis about value creation. Each offers an opportunity to gather evidence rather than simply implement solutions.

The transformation begins with a simple commitment: to treat your most important initiatives as experiments designed to test hypotheses about value creation. This shift in thinking - from implementation to experimentation - creates immediate improvements in decision quality while building long-term organizational capabilities.

Your success as a leader increasingly depends on your organization's ability to navigate uncertainty with confidence. Evidence-based management turns uncertainty from a threat into a competitive advantage by creating systematic approaches for learning and adaptation.

This isn't about perfecting measurement or eliminating risk. It's about building capabilities that enable your organization to succeed precisely because the path forward isn't entirely clear. In an industry where change is the only constant, these capabilities may be the most important competitive advantage you can develop.

The time to begin is now. Your customers, your employees, and your stakeholders are counting on your ability to create genuine value in an increasingly complex world. Evidence-Based Management provides the framework. The commitment to begin is yours.

Five Actions to Start Your Evidence-Based Transformation

Transform One Initiative into an Experiment

Select your most important current initiative. Write down the hypothesis it represents about value creation. Define how you'll measure whether that value materializes.

Measure One Key Value Area

Choose current value, unrealized value, ability to innovate, or time-to-market. Identify three specific indicators that would reveal your organization's performance in this area.

Establish Goal-Evidence Alignment

Review your top three organizational goals. For each goal, identify what customer outcome would indicate success and how you'll measure progress toward that outcome.

Create Learning Cycles

Schedule monthly one-hour sessions to review evidence from recent initiatives, extract learning, and adapt approaches based on results.

Model Evidence-Based Thinking

In your next leadership decision, explicitly state your hypothesis, define success criteria, and commit to measuring results objectively.

TEMPLATES

The competitive advantage created by evidence-based capabilities compounds over time. Organizations that learn faster, adapt quicker, and focus more clearly on value creation pull ahead of competitors still operating with assumption-based approaches. In rapidly changing markets, this advantage often proves decisive.

10

CHAPTER

Getting Your Strategy Done

Imagine this scenario: you sit in a conference room, reviewing your annual performance as a regional vice president for a growing tech company. The spreadsheet on your laptop shows the cold reality of those carefully crafted goals that determined your compensation just twelve months earlier.

The numbers don't lie, but they tell a story you never expected.

Initiative after initiative marked "postponed" or "canceled." The data lake project that was supposed to revolutionize operations? No clear status. The new product line that would capture emerging markets? Quietly pushed out three quarters. The strategic partnership that promised to expand your customer base? Stuck between departments.

I stared at that screen, experiencing what I can only describe as professional breakdown. How do you reconcile a year of dedicated effort with a portfolio of abandoned strategies? More importantly, how do you prevent this from happening again?

This wasn't just my story - it's the untold narrative playing out in corporations across the tech sector. The harsh truth that most executives discover, usually too late, is that strategy formulation represents only half the battle. The other half - execution - determines whether your carefully crafted plans become market-changing realities or expensive lessons in corporate frustration.

John Charles Salak captured this perfectly: "Failures are divided into two classes - those who thought and never did, and those who did and never thought." But there's a third class he didn't mention: those who thought brilliantly, planned meticulously, and still watched their strategies crumble during execution.

Here's what shocked me most during that business review: we weren't dealing with bad strategies. Our market analysis was solid, our competitive positioning was sound, and our financial projections were realistic. We had smart people, adequate resources, and executive support. Yet somehow, the gap between intention and implementation had swallowed millions of dollars and countless hours of effort.

The Brutal Statistics

The statistics paint an even grimmer picture. The number one concern of CEOs - ranked higher than market competition, regulatory changes, or technological disruption - is failing strategy execution. When surveyed, **70% of strategists admit they're concerned about their ability to actually close the strategy execution gap**. Only **10% of strategic plans ever reach full implementation**.

Let that sink in for a moment. **Nine out of ten strategic initiatives fail not because of poor thinking, but because of poor execution.**

Companies that master strategy execution, however, increase profitability by **77%**. They don't just survive market turbulence; they thrive by turning strategic vision into operational reality. They've cracked the code that transforms boardroom discussions into marketplace dominance.

The question isn't whether you have a good strategy - most tech leaders do. The question is whether you have a system for executing that strategy consistently, adaptively, and successfully. Whether you can bridge the gap between what you plan to do and what finally gets done.

What I learned from that eye-opening business review is that strategy execution isn't an art - it's a system. A learnable, repeatable, scalable system that can transform your organization's ability to turn strategic intent into measurable results.

The system isn't complicated, but it is comprehensive. It requires disciplined attention to several interconnected elements that work together to create "execution momentum" - the organizational force that propels strategies from concept to completion.

Element 1:

Make Sure Everyone's Actually Working on the Same Thing

Consider Martina, CTO of a mid-sized fintech company, who spent three months developing a comprehensive digital transformation strategy. The board approved it enthusiastically. The executive team championed it publicly. The budget was allocated generously. Six months later, Martina discovered that **67% of her teams couldn't explain how their daily work connected to the transformation goals**.

This scenario plays out with disturbing frequency across the tech sector. Research reveals that **74% of executives admit their strategies aren't well-translated into concrete actions**. Meanwhile, **79% express concern that their organizations don't allocate sufficient resources to implement their strategies effectively**.

Most leaders assume that clarity at the executive level automatically translates to clarity at the operational level. This assumption kills more strategies than market competition ever will.

True alignment begins with "strategic translation" - the disciplined process of converting high-level objectives into specific, actionable, and measurable work streams. This isn't about creating more documentation; it's about building bridges between strategic thinking and operational execution.

Start with Ruthless Priority Definition

If everything is important, nothing is important. Successful companies focus their execution energy on a limited number of strategic initiatives - typically three to five major objectives that can realistically be achieved within the planning timeframe. Each priority must pass the "elevator test": Can you explain its importance and impact in thirty seconds or less?

Make Your Budget Match Your Strategy

Resource allocation must match strategic priorities. Too many organizations treat budgeting and strategic planning as separate exercises, then wonder why their most important initiatives remain chronically under-resourced. Companies that excel at execution align their spending with their strategy from day one. They ask critical questions early:

- What technology investments will these objectives require?
- Which skill sets do we need to develop or acquire?
- How much time should our best people dedicate to strategic work versus operational maintenance?

Build Communication Architecture

The communication architecture you build around your strategy determines whether alignment happens by accident or by design.

High-performing executives spend **12% more time creating alignment** through frequent, structured communication. They don't just announce strategies; they embed them into regular management rhythms, team meetings, and individual performance discussions.

When Microsoft shifted from software licensing to cloud services, they didn't just change their product strategy - they redesigned their entire execution system. Teams were reorganized around cloud objectives. Compensation structures were aligned with subscription metrics. Communication rhythms were restructured to emphasize customer success over feature delivery. Performance reviews were reframed to reward collaboration over individual achievement.

The transformation worked because they recognized that strategic shifts require execution shifts. New strategies demand new ways of working, measuring, and rewarding progress.

When alignment is done correctly, it creates organizational coherence. Teams understand not just what they're supposed to do, but why their work matters to the company's larger ambitions. Resources flow toward high-impact activities. Decision-making accelerates because everyone shares a common understanding of priorities and success metrics.

Element 2:

Make Sure Everyone Actually Knows What the Priorities Are

During a quarterly business review at a software company, I watched the CEO passionately describe the organization's growth strategy to a room of department heads. Afterward, I asked each attendee to write down the company's top three priorities. The results were shocking - no two people listed identical priorities, and several couldn't name even one strategic objective.

This communication crisis isn't unique to smaller companies. Research shows that **95% of employees are unaware of or don't understand their organization's strategy**. Even more troubling, **67% of employees don't understand how new growth initiatives impact their individual work**. When the people doing the work don't understand the strategy, execution becomes impossible.

Contextual Cascading

Effective communication in strategy execution goes far beyond traditional corporate messaging. It requires "contextual cascading" - the art of translating strategic priorities into language and examples that resonate at every organizational level:

- Engineers need to understand how their code releases support strategic objectives
- Sales teams need clarity on which opportunities align with company priorities
- Customer success managers need insight into how their retention efforts connect to broader growth goals

Executives who excel at strategy execution establish regular communication rhythms that keep strategy visible and relevant:

- **Weekly team meetings** include strategic context
- **Monthly reviews** connect operational metrics to strategic progress
- **Quarterly sessions** provide opportunities for feedback and course correction

Measure Outcomes, Not Activities

Communication alone isn't enough. You need to measure what matters. Too many organizations fall into the activity trap - tracking how busy people are rather than how much progress they're making toward strategic objectives.

This is where frameworks like Objectives and Key Results become transformational. Instead of measuring activities, you measure outcomes. Instead of counting hours worked, you count value created. Instead of tracking tasks completed, you track goals achieved.

Think about how this works in practice. Suppose your strategy includes expanding into the Middle East market. Rather than measuring activities like "attended trade shows" or "created marketing materials," you define clear outcomes:

- Host fifteen events with prospective customers by end of Q2
- Hire twelve employees to support operations by end of Q3
- Complete fifty transactions in your Middle East region by end of Q3

The magic happens when you connect individual work to these strategic outcomes. Teams develop sub-objectives that ladder up to company goals. Individuals collaborate with their managers to set personal objectives that contribute to team success.

This approach transforms motivation and accountability. When people can see direct connections between their efforts and strategic success, engagement increases dramatically. When progress is visible and measurable, course corrections happen naturally rather than through management intervention.

At Google, all employee objectives and key results are visible across the entire organization. This radical transparency creates collaborative accountability. Teams can see how their work connects to other departments' efforts. Individuals understand how their contributions fit into larger strategic initiatives. Leaders gain real-time visibility into organizational progress.

Element 3:

Make Progress Visible and Fix Problems Fast

Netflix transformed entertainment by mastering something that most companies struggle with: making progress transparent and adjusting quickly when reality diverges from plans. Their transition from DVD-by-mail to streaming to content creation involved countless strategic pivots, each informed by real-time data about customer behavior, market conditions, and competitive dynamics.

This agility didn't happen by accident. It emerged from systematic attention to what high-performing teams do differently: they spend **14% more time measuring progress** against strategic goals, then adjusting resources in response to what they learn.

Three Critical Questions

Making progress visible requires answering three fundamental questions during strategy execution planning:

1. **What data do we need** to track progress toward objectives and key results?
2. **Who will gather, interpret, and share** these numbers?
3. **How will we share progress** with everyone involved?

The first question demands careful consideration. Not all data is useful data. Effective measurement focuses on **leading indicators** - metrics that predict future success - rather than lagging indicators that only confirm what already happened.

If your objective involves improving customer retention, tracking customer engagement scores and support ticket resolution times provides more actionable insights than simply monitoring churn rates after customers have already left.

The second question involves creating accountability without bureaucracy. Someone needs responsibility for collecting, analyzing, and sharing progress data, but this shouldn't become a full-time job for multiple people. The most effective approach involves integrating measurement into existing workflows rather than creating parallel reporting systems.

The third question touches on organizational psychology. Transparency about progress - including lack of progress - requires psychological safety. Teams need confidence that sharing accurate information, even when it reveals problems, will lead to support and problem-solving rather than blame and punishment.

Intelligent Responsiveness

Visibility without action becomes mere performance theater. The real value emerges when organizations develop "intelligent responsiveness" - the ability to interpret progress data and adjust course quickly when needed.

This responsiveness manifests in several ways:

- **Resource reallocation** happens rapidly when data reveals that certain initiatives are progressing faster or slower than anticipated
- **Timeline adjustments** occur before delays become crises
- **Strategic emphasis shifts** when market feedback indicates that customer needs have evolved

Think of a large fleet of small ships, rather than a small fleet of large ships. You need distributed decision-making carried out by capable people you can trust. There's no time to run every move by senior leadership. Empower teams to act within their areas of expertise.

The key insight is that agility and strategic discipline aren't opposing forces - they're complementary capabilities. Strong strategic frameworks provide the foundation that makes rapid adaptation possible. When everyone understands the destination and the success metrics, course corrections become collaborative decisions rather than executive mandates.

Element 4:

Embrace Learning Over Being Right

The strategy you implement today will require significant adaptation tomorrow. Markets evolve, technologies advance, customer needs shift, and competitive landscapes transform. Companies that treat strategy execution as a fixed process - a series of predetermined steps leading to predictable outcomes - inevitably struggle when reality diverges from their plans.

Carol Dweck's groundbreaking research on growth mindset reveals why some organizations thrive during uncertainty while others falter. Organizations with growth mindsets see setbacks as learning opportunities, embrace challenges as chances to improve, and treat failure as valuable data rather than final judgment.

From Fixed to Growth

This mindset shift transforms how teams approach strategy execution:

- Instead of rigidly following predetermined plans, they **experiment intelligently**
- Instead of viewing obstacles as threats, they **treat them as puzzles to solve**
- Instead of punishing mistakes, they **celebrate intelligent failures** that generate useful insights

Consider how this plays out in practice. A software company pursuing market expansion discovers that their initial customer acquisition strategy isn't generating expected results. A fixed mindset organization might persist with the original plan, hoping more effort will overcome the obstacles. A growth mindset organization investigates why the strategy isn't working, experiments with alternative approaches, and adapts their tactics based on what they learn.

The difference in outcomes is profound. Growth mindset organizations develop resilience and adaptability that enable them to navigate uncertainty successfully. They build learning capabilities that make them stronger over time. They create cultures where innovation flourishes because people feel safe to experiment and learn from failures.

Building Growth Mindset into Execution

Integrating growth mindset into strategy execution requires intentional effort:

Teach it:

Leadership development and employee onboarding should emphasize that strategic execution is an iterative process of experimentation and learning, not a linear progression from planning to results.

Reinforce it:

Recognition and reward systems need to celebrate intelligent experiments, even when they don't produce intended results. Acknowledge teams that adapt quickly to changing circumstances.

Measure it:

Collect employee feedback about how safe they feel making mistakes and offering new ideas, rather than feeling punished for mistakes or ignored for being innovative.

Perhaps most importantly, growth mindset organizations develop "execution intelligence" - the ability to sense when strategies need adjustment and respond quickly with creative solutions. This intelligence becomes a sustainable competitive advantage that compounds over time.

Making It All Work Together

Strategy execution transforms from organizational challenge to competitive advantage when leaders approach it as a systematic discipline rather than a hopeful activity. The companies that consistently translate strategic vision into marketplace results don't rely on inspiration or heroic effort - they build execution systems that work regardless of individual personalities or market conditions.

The elements we've explored create a reinforcing cycle of execution excellence:

- **Strategic alignment** ensures that effort flows toward high-impact activities
- **Clear communication** keeps everyone moving in the same direction
- **Outcome-focused measurement** provides real-time feedback about progress
- **Transparent reporting** enables rapid course correction
- **Growth mindset** creates resilience and adaptability

These elements generate execution momentum that compounds over time.

The transformation isn't immediate, but it's inevitable when applied consistently. Organizations report increased employee engagement as people understand how their work contributes to strategic success. Leaders experience reduced frustration as strategies get implemented. Shareholders see improved returns as strategic investments generate intended results.

Think about the alternative. Without systematic execution, even brilliant strategies become expensive exercises in organizational frustration. Teams work harder but accomplish less. Resources get scattered across competing priorities. Innovation slows because people can't see connections between their efforts and meaningful outcomes.

The most successful tech companies don't accept this status quo. They invest in building execution capabilities that deliver consistent results. They create organizational muscle memory that turns strategy into action automatically, efficiently, and effectively.

Your Choice

The choice facing every tech leader is simple: continue accepting the **90% failure rate** that characterizes most strategic initiatives or invest in building execution capabilities that deliver consistent results. The companies that choose the latter don't just survive market turbulence - they create the turbulence that their competitors struggle to navigate.

Your execution system becomes your competitive moat. While competitors struggle to translate vision into reality, you're already implementing your next strategic advantage. While others debate priorities in endless meetings, your teams are creating measurable progress toward clear objectives.

The system works, but only when you work the system consistently and deliberately.

Five Actions to Strengthen Your Strategy Execution

Conduct an Alignment Audit

Survey your team to identify gaps between strategic priorities and daily activities, then create specific action plans to close these gaps.

Establish Weekly Execution Reviews

Implement brief, structured meetings focused solely on strategic progress, obstacles, and resource needs.

Define Three Outcome-Based Metrics

Replace activity tracking with results measurement that directly connects to your most important strategic objectives.

Create Transparency Dashboards

Make strategic progress visible across your organization through shared metrics and regular communication.

Implement Learning Protocols

Establish formal processes for capturing lessons from both successes and failures, then applying these insights to improve future execution.

TEMPLATES

The companies that master strategy execution don't just survive - they define the future of their industries. The framework is clear, the tools are available, and the choice is yours. The question isn't whether you can build better execution capabilities - it's whether you will.

11

CHAPTER

Using Technology to Win

The boardroom in London Stratford was electric with anticipation. Two months after acquiring Beanstack Solutions, our leadership team gathered to review the integration results. The numbers should have been cause for celebration - we'd successfully consolidated operations, reduced overhead, and achieved the cost savings promised to shareholders. Yet something felt profoundly wrong.

"Marketing lead generation is down 60%," announced Christian, our CRO, his voice cutting through the congratulatory atmosphere like a blade. "Conversion rates have plummeted to below industry average, and we've lost Beanstack's top marketing professionals in the past month."

The silence that followed was deafening. Six months earlier, Beanstack had been our acquisition target precisely because of their extraordinary marketing efficiency. Their inbound lead generation machine converted prospects at rates that made industry veterans weep with envy. Their sophisticated marketing technology stack - a carefully orchestrated symphony of tools, platforms, and automated workflows - had been the secret weapon that made a 100-person company outperform marketing teams three times their size.

Then we made what seemed like a rational business decision. Our Chief Marketing Officer, armed with consultants and cost-reduction mandates, decided to "drive synergies" by consolidating Beanstack's marketing technology onto our corporate standard platforms. After all, why pay for duplicate systems when we could achieve economies of scale?

The sophisticated marketing stack that Beanstack had spent years optimizing was dismantled within weeks. Their custom-configured CRM integrations, finely tuned attribution models, and automated nurture sequences - all replaced with our "proven" corporate tools. The marketing experts who understood the intricate relationships between these systems watched helplessly as their carefully crafted engine was torn apart and rebuilt with generic components.

The exodus began immediately. When you strip away the tools that make professionals exceptional at their craft, you don't just lose efficiency - you lose the people who created that efficiency. The institutional knowledge walked out the door along with the frustrated employees, leaving us with inferior results and a harsh lesson in the true cost of technology decisions.

This experience taught me something fundamental about modern business success: **technology isn't only about tools and systems. It's about enabling human potential and amplifying organizational capabilities.** When you make technology decisions purely from a cost perspective, you don't just change software - you dismantle competitive advantages that took years to build.

Your Tech Stack Is Your Nervous System

At its core, a technology stack represents far more than the sum of its digital parts. Think of it as the nervous system of your organization - a sophisticated network of programming languages, frameworks, tools, and infrastructure that enables every business function to operate at peak performance. Like the human nervous system, when this technological backbone functions seamlessly, it's nearly invisible. But when it's disrupted or poorly designed, the entire organism suffers.

Your technology stack consists of distinct layers:

Foundation layer: Hardware infrastructure, networks, and basic platforms

Application layer: Software tools your teams use daily

Data layer: Information flow and storage management

Security layer: Protection from threats and compliance assurance

Integration layer: Ensures all components communicate effectively

But here's what most executives miss: **the real power of a technology stack isn't in individual tools - it's in the relationships between them.** When Beanstack's marketing team had configured their stack, they hadn't just selected good software. They'd created an ecosystem where lead scoring algorithms fed seamlessly into email automation, where website behavior triggered personalized content delivery and where sales conversations automatically informed marketing optimization.

The modern technology stack serves as the foundation and the accelerator of business growth. It determines not only what your organization can accomplish but how quickly and efficiently you can accomplish it. In today's hyper-competitive marketplace, the quality of your technology decisions often determines whether you're setting the pace or struggling to keep up.

Why Your Tech Stack Determines Everything

Imagine walking into two different software companies on the same day. In the first office, developers spend hours manually deploying code, marketers wrestle with disconnected systems that don't talk to each other, and customer service representatives toggle between seven different applications to resolve a single inquiry. Frustration permeates the air like a fog.

The second company feels entirely different. Teams move with fluid efficiency, data flows seamlessly between departments, and employees focus on creative problem-solving rather than fighting their tools. The difference isn't talent, culture, or even strategy - it's the quality of the technology foundation supporting every individual's effort.

This stark contrast shows a crucial truth: **every role and function within your organization has specific goals and tasks that can either be elevated by best-in-class technology or hindered by mediocre solutions.** The companies that consistently outperform their competitors understand that technology isn't an expense center - it's a strategic multiplier that amplifies human potential.

The Customer-Employee-Centric Approach

Best-in-class organizations approach technology decisions with a fundamental principle: center everything around how to best support customers and employees. This approach drives decisions that might seem counterintuitive from a pure cost perspective but deliver exponential returns in performance and satisfaction.

Consider how Netflix revolutionized entertainment not by creating better content initially but by building technology that eliminated friction from the viewing experience. Their recommendation algorithms, streaming infrastructure, and user interface innovations focused relentlessly on making it easier for customers to discover and enjoy content. Simultaneously, they equipped their content creators and data scientists with sophisticated tools that enabled unprecedented insights into viewer preferences.

The Consolidation Trap

Yet far too many organizations fall into the consolidation trap that nearly destroyed our Beanstack acquisition. The allure of "one platform to rule them all" promises simplicity and cost savings, but this approach fundamentally misunderstands how modern work happens.

Different functions require different capabilities:

- Your sales team needs CRM features that your HR department finds irrelevant
- Your marketing department requires automation sophistication that would overwhelm your finance team
- Your engineering team needs development tools that would confuse your accounting staff

When you force disparate functions onto identical platforms purely for cost savings, you're essentially asking a surgeon to perform operations with the same tools a carpenter uses to build houses. Both are skilled professionals, but their craft requires specialized instruments optimized for their specific challenges.

The Talent Drain

The most damaging consequence of over-consolidation isn't just reduced efficiency - it's the talent drain that follows. **High-performing professionals gravitate toward organizations that provide them with the tools necessary to excel.** When you downgrade their technology capabilities, you're not simply reducing productivity; you're sending a clear message about how much you value their contributions.

Research from MIT's Sloan School of Management reveals that companies with highly aligned IT and business functions achieve:

- **20% faster time-to-market** for new products and services
- **25% higher employee satisfaction** scores
- **Significantly lower turnover rates** among high-performing team members

Mapping Technology to Your Business Functions

The pace of technological evolution has reached unprecedented speed. A Stanford study tracking enterprise software adoption found that **breakthrough technologies now move from early adopter to mainstream implementation in eighteen months** - half the time it took just five years ago. With artificial intelligence accelerating innovation cycles even further, the window for competitive advantage continues to shrink.

Smart organizations have abandoned the one-size-fits-all mentality in favor of "functional technology optimization." This approach recognizes that different business areas require fundamentally different technological capabilities, even within the same company.

Consider Amazon's technological architecture:

- Their retail division operates on sophisticated inventory management and recommendation systems
- Their cloud services division (AWS) requires entirely different infrastructure focused on scalability and security
- Their streaming service needs content delivery optimization and viewer analytics

Attempting to run AWS on the retail division's technology stack would be like trying to perform brain surgery with kitchen utensils - theoretically possible but practically disastrous.

Key Technology Categories

Modern organizations typically require specialized technology strategies across several key areas:

Strategic Management Solutions

- Support ideation processes and objective setting
- Enable investment and capacity planning
- Provide strategic portfolio management
- Transform decision-making from intuition to data-driven insights

Infrastructure Technology

- Hardware, software, networks, and data centers
- Creates the reliable backbone that enables other investments to deliver value
- Determines whether expensive applications can perform as promised

Application Technology

- Software tools and platforms for daily work
- Varies dramatically across functions
- Marketing: automation platforms, attribution modeling, content management
- Sales: CRM capabilities, prospecting tools, performance analytics
- Development: integrated environments, testing frameworks, deployment automation

Data and Information Management

- Storage, security, and leverage of information
- Transforms data from byproduct to strategic asset
- Enables insights that drive competitive advantages

Security and Compliance

- Protects company and customer data
- Ensures regulatory requirements are met
- Prevents breaches that destroy customer trust

Marketing Technology

- Directly impacts revenue generation
- Determines customer acquisition costs and conversion rates
- Enables deep understanding of ideal customer profiles

The Two High-Impact Domains

While every system contributes to organizational performance, research shows that **70% of digital investments are destined to fail** before you even write the first check. The primary cause? The absence of strategic approaches that align technology investments with business outcomes.

Two domains consistently emerge as game-changers for software and IT companies: **strategic management technology** and **marketing technology stacks**.

Strategic Management Technology

Strategic management technology represents the nervous system of organizational decision-making. These systems support the entire lifecycle of strategic thinking - from initial ideation through objective setting, investment planning, capacity allocation, and portfolio management.

The impact extends far beyond process improvement:

- **80% reductions in funding process timelines** for new initiatives
- **Better decisions made faster** with real-time insights
- **35% faster product development cycles**
- **28% improvement in successful market entry rates**

Consider a mid-market software company that implemented comprehensive strategic management technology two years ago. Previously, their quarterly planning cycles consumed six weeks of senior leadership time, often resulting in resource allocation decisions based on incomplete information. Today, those same planning cycles require less than one week, and decisions are made with unprecedented visibility into dependencies, resource constraints, and expected outcomes.

Strategic management technology becomes increasingly critical as organizations grow. Small companies can rely on informal coordination and leadership intuition. But as complexity increases - more products, more markets, more stakeholders - the human capacity to process strategic information becomes the limiting factor.

Marketing Technology Stacks

Marketing technology stacks represent the second area of disproportionate impact, particularly for growth-focused software companies. **Your marketing stack determines how efficiently and**

effectively you communicate value to prospective customers. More crucially, it defines your customer acquisition economics - the fundamental metrics that determine whether your business model is sustainable and scalable.

The sophistication of your marketing technology directly correlates with your ability to identify, attract, and convert ideal customers. Companies with optimized marketing stacks consistently achieve:

- **Lower customer acquisition costs**
- **Higher conversion rates**
- **Greater customer lifetime value**

Research from the Marketing Technology Institute shows that companies with highly integrated marketing stacks achieve:

- **39% higher lead conversion rates**
- **37% lower customer acquisition costs**

Netflix's marketing technology exemplifies this principle. Their recommendation algorithms don't just suggest content; they create personalized marketing experiences that increase engagement and reduce churn. Their sophisticated attribution modeling enables precise measurement of marketing effectiveness across channels.

But here's what most executives miss: **marketing technology isn't just about campaign execution.** Advanced marketing stacks provide deep insights into customer behavior, market dynamics, and competitive positioning. They become intelligence gathering systems that inform product development, pricing strategies, and market expansion decisions.

Building Your Technology Strategy Framework

Most technology strategies fail not because of poor execution, but because they lack a systematic approach to planning and implementation. Like constructing a building without blueprints, organizations that skip strategic frameworks often find themselves with expensive technology investments that don't deliver expected business outcomes.

A robust technology strategy framework provides the scaffolding for making informed decisions about technological investments. The most successful software and IT companies follow a disciplined seven-component framework:

1. Objective Setting

Clearly define your organization's strategic goals and identify how technology can support those objectives. This isn't about listing every possible technological improvement. Instead, it requires honest assessment of your most critical business challenges and growth opportunities.

Ask uncomfortable questions:

- Why are your current systems inadequate for achieving strategic goals?
- What capabilities would give you significant competitive advantages?

- How do your technology limitations currently constrain business growth?

2. Technology Assessment

Comprehensively examine your current technological landscape and the broader market. Create detailed inventories of existing technology assets, evaluate their effectiveness, and identify emerging technologies that might offer competitive opportunities.

Research from Gartner indicates that **60% of organizations significantly underestimate the limitations of their current systems and the potential impact of emerging technologies.**

3. Gap Analysis

Systematically compare current capabilities with strategic requirements. Identify specific deficiencies in hardware, software, data management, security, skills, or integration capabilities.

The most valuable gap analyses examine not just what you lack but why those gaps exist:

- Do funding constraints limit technology investments?
- Are organizational silos preventing integrated solutions?
- Has rapid growth outpaced infrastructure development?

4. Solution Identification

Explore potential approaches to address identified gaps. This might include purchasing new technology, upgrading existing systems, outsourcing specific functions, developing internal capabilities, or partnering with technology providers.

Smart solution identification considers:

- Total cost of ownership
- Implementation complexity
- Organizational change requirements
- Long-term scalability

5. Implementation Planning

Create detailed roadmaps for deploying identified solutions. Effective plans include realistic timelines, resource requirements, responsibility assignments, and key performance indicators for measuring progress.

Implementation planning must account for organizational change management, not just technical deployment:

- How will you train users?
- What processes need modification?
- How will you maintain productivity during transitions?

6. Execution

Implement plans while monitoring progress against established KPIs and adjusting approaches based on feedback and changing conditions. This requires continuous attention and course correction as implementation reveals unexpected challenges or opportunities.

7. Review and Evaluation

Ensure technology strategies remain aligned with evolving business needs, technological developments, and lessons learned from implementation. Regular strategic reviews prevent technology decisions from becoming legacy constraints on future growth.

Staying Ahead of the Curve

The morning Steve Jobs unveiled the iPhone, executives at BlackBerry, Nokia, and Motorola woke up in a completely different competitive landscape. Overnight, the rules of mobile communication shifted so dramatically that companies with decades of market leadership found themselves scrambling to understand technologies they'd dismissed as irrelevant just months earlier.

Today's breakthrough becomes tomorrow's baseline expectation, and what seems impossible in January often becomes standard practice by December. The introduction of artificial intelligence has amplified this acceleration exponentially, creating innovation cycles that would have seemed science fiction merely five years ago.

Outcome-First Approach

Yet here's the critical insight most organizations miss: **implementing new technology without clear expected goals represents one of the fastest paths to wasted resources and organizational confusion.** Before evaluating any technological advancement, successful leaders establish specific outcomes they want to achieve:

- Are you trying to reduce operational costs?
- Improve customer satisfaction scores?
- Accelerate product development cycles?
- Enable new revenue streams?

This outcome-first approach prevents the common trap of adopting impressive technologies that don't address actual business challenges. The most sophisticated AI implementation becomes worthless if it doesn't solve real problems or create meaningful advantages.

Consider how Zoom approached video conferencing technology. While competitors focused on adding features and improving technical specifications, **Zoom obsessed over a single outcome: making video meetings so simple and reliable that people would prefer them to phone calls.** This clarity of purpose guided every technological decision.

The result? When the pandemic forced global remote work adoption, Zoom was positioned to become essential business infrastructure because their technology strategy aligned perfectly with what customers needed.

Building Technological Agility

Staying current requires balancing systematic monitoring with strategic focus. The most effective approach involves creating organizational learning systems rather than relying on individual awareness:

- **Assign team members** to track developments in specific technological areas
- **Establish relationships** with technology vendors, research institutions, and industry analysts
- **Participate in relevant conferences** and professional associations
- **Run pilot programs** with limited scope and clear success metrics
- **Test emerging solutions** with non-critical applications before enterprise-wide implementations

The goal isn't adopting every innovation - it's developing organizational capabilities for rapid technological evolution. Companies that excel at this develop "technological agility" - the ability to quickly assess, experiment with, and implement beneficial technologies while avoiding costly mistakes with unproven solutions.

Your Technology Future

Remember the lesson from our Beanstack acquisition: **choosing the right technology stack represents far more than technical**

decision-making. It's fundamentally strategic, setting direction for your organization's competitive positioning, operational efficiency, and growth potential.

The companies that consistently outperform competitors don't just use better technology - they make better technology decisions. They understand that every technological choice either amplifies human potential or constrains it. They recognize that technology stacks create compounding advantages when properly designed and implemented.

Your technology strategy determines whether your organization sets the pace in your industry or struggles to keep up with more technologically sophisticated competitors. The framework we've explored provides the foundation for making these critical decisions systematically rather than reactively.

Five Immediate Action Steps

Conduct a Technology Audit

Within the next thirty days, inventory every significant technology system your organization uses. Evaluate each system's alignment with current business objectives and identify obvious gaps or redundancies. Focus particularly on systems that constrain rather than enable performance.

Establish Functional Technology Partnerships

Create formal collaboration between your IT department and each major business function. Assign technology advocates within marketing, sales, operations, finance and other key areas that can bridge between technical capabilities and business requirements.

Define Technology Success Metrics

For each major technology investment, establish clear, measurable outcomes you expect to achieve. Move beyond technical metrics like uptime or processing speed to business impact measures like customer acquisition costs, employee productivity, or revenue per customer.

Create an Innovation Pipeline

Allocate 10 to 15% of your technology budget specifically for experimenting with emerging technologies. Run controlled pilots with new solutions before committing to full implementations. This approach reduces risk while ensuring you don't miss breakthrough opportunities.

Schedule Quarterly Technology Strategy Reviews

Implement regular sessions to evaluate technology performance against business objectives, assess new opportunities, and adjust your technology roadmap based on changing business needs and market conditions. Make these reviews as rigorous and strategic as your financial planning sessions.

The difference between technology leaders and technology laggards isn't access to better tools - it's systematic approaches to making technology decisions that create sustainable competitive advantages. Your next technology choice could be the decision that defines your organization's future.

TEMPLATES

12

CHAPTER

Your Path Forward - Putting It All Together

We started this journey with a simple observation: most business advice sounds great in theory but falls apart when you try to apply it in the real world. Too much of what passes for "strategy" is wishful thinking dressed up in corporate jargon. Too many "proven frameworks" work great for the companies that created them but fail miserably when you try to implement them in your unique situation.

That's why this book has been different. Every chapter, every framework, every piece of advice has been tested in the trenches of real companies facing real challenges. We've talked about failures as much as successes, because that's where the real learning happens.

Now, as we wrap up this journey, let's step back and see how all these pieces fit together into a complete system for building and scaling successful technology companies.

The Foundation: Know Where You're Going and Who You're Serving

Everything starts with clarity. Not the kind of fake clarity that comes from beautiful PowerPoint presentations, but the bone-deep clarity that only comes from asking hard questions and giving yourself honest answers.

Your North Star Vision (Chapter 4) isn't just a nice-to-have statement for your website. It's your decision-making filter, your team alignment tool, and your competitive advantage rolled into one. When everyone in your organization understands not just what you're building but why it matters and where you're ultimately heading, magical things start to happen. Decisions get made faster. Teams collaborate better. People stay motivated even when things get tough.

But a vision without customers is just a daydream. **Understanding Your Ideal Customer** (Chapter 5) with surgical precision transforms everything about how you operate. When you know exactly who you're serving, what they really need (not what they say they need), and how they make decisions, you stop wasting time on features nobody wants and start building things people can't live without.

The companies that dominate their markets don't simply have good products - they have deep, almost intimate understanding of their customers' real problems and motivations. They know their customers better than their customers know themselves.

The Engine: Getting the Right People Working the Right Way

With clarity on direction and customers, you need the engine that will get you there. This is where most companies stumble. They either hire the wrong people, organize the right people badly, or give good people terrible tools and processes.

Getting the Right People in the Right Jobs (Chapter 6) isn't just about hiring smart people - it's about understanding that different roles need different personality types, different motivations, and different working styles. The traits that make someone an exceptional individual contributor might make them a terrible manager. The skills that work in a startup environment might be all wrong for a scaled company.

More importantly, it's about creating teams where the whole is greater than the sum of its parts. Where different personality types complement rather than clash with each other. Where people understand not just their own role, but how their work connects to everyone else's success.

But even the best people will fail if you organize them wrong. **Designing an Agile Organization** (Chapter 7) showed us that the traditional corporate structure - with its matrices, hierarchies, and endless approval chains - is fundamentally incompatible with the speed and adaptability that modern markets demand.

The future belongs to organizations that can combine the agility of a startup with the resources of an enterprise. Small, autonomous teams that own outcomes, not just activities. Leaders who serve their teams rather than command them. Structures that evolve as quickly as the market conditions they're trying to navigate.

The System: How You Get Things Done

Having great people organized well is still not enough if you don't have systems that work. This is where the rubber meets the road - where strategy either becomes reality or dies in a pile of good intentions.

Your Operating Model (Chapter 8) determines whether you're built for the project mindset (slow, predictable, plan-driven) or the product mindset (fast, adaptive, outcome-driven). The companies winning today have moved from asking "How can we execute this plan?" to asking "How can we solve this problem and create this value?"

This isn't just a philosophical difference - it's a practical one with massive implications for how you organize work, measure success, and adapt to change. Product-minded organizations don't just respond to market changes; they create them.

But good operating models need good information to work properly. **Making Decisions Based on What Works** (Chapter 9) taught us that being "data-driven" isn't enough - you need to be evidence-driven. You need systems that tell you not just what happened but whether what happened created the value you intended.

The best organizations don't just collect data; they design experiments. They don't merely measure activity; they measure outcomes. They don't only track what they did; they track whether what they did worked.

The Execution: From Strategy to Results

All the clarity, people, and systems in the world won't help you if you can't execute consistently. This is where most strategies go to die - not because they were bad strategies, but because the organization couldn't bridge the gap between intention and implementation.

Getting Your Strategy Done (Chapter 10) revealed the brutal truth: 90% of strategic initiatives fail not because of poor thinking, but because of poor execution. The companies that consistently turn strategy into results have built systematic approaches to execution that work regardless of individual personalities or market conditions.

They ensure everyone knows what the priorities are and how their work connects to strategic success. They make progress visible and fix problems fast. They treat obstacles as puzzles to solve rather than excuses for failure.

Finally, **Using Technology to Win** (Chapter 11) showed us that in our digital-first world, your technology choices either amplify your competitive advantages or constrain them. The organizations winning today don't just use technology - they think strategically about technology. They understand that the right tech stack can make good people great and great people unstoppable.

How It All Fits Together

Here's what makes this approach different from most business advice: these aren't separate initiatives you implement one by one. They're interconnected elements of a complete system that reinforces itself:

- **Your vision** guides your customer selection and people decisions
- **Your ideal customer understanding** shapes your operating model and technology choices
- **Your people and team structure** determines what strategies you can execute
- **Your operating model** enables your evidence-based decision making
- **Your execution system** brings your vision to life through your people
- **Your technology** amplifies everything else you do

When these elements work together, they create "competitive momentum" - the kind of self-reinforcing advantages that are almost impossible for competitors to copy because they're not built on any single innovation or insight, but on how well all the pieces work together.

The Companies That Get This Right

Look at the companies that consistently outperform their competitors across economic cycles and market changes. Amazon didn't become dominant because they were first to market in e-commerce. They won because they built a complete system: obsessive customer focus, long-term vision, operational excellence, technology that scales, people who can execute, and the ability to adapt faster than anyone else.

Netflix didn't just get lucky with streaming. They systematically built capabilities in content recommendation, user experience, data analytics, content creation, and global distribution. Each capability reinforced the others.

These companies understand something that their competitors miss: sustainable competitive advantage doesn't come from being better at one thing. It comes from being systematically better at how all the important things work together.

Your Choice

As a leader in today's technology landscape, you face a choice. You can continue operating the way most companies do - managing each challenge as it arises, implementing best practices one at a time, hoping that somehow all the pieces will eventually come together.

Or you can take a systematic approach. You can build your organization as an integrated system where every element reinforces every other element. Where your vision drives your customer focus, which shapes your people decisions, which enables your operating model, which powers your execution system, which delivers results that validate your vision.

The first approach might work when markets are stable and competition is predictable. But in our world of constant change and accelerating innovation, systematic thinking isn't just better - it's necessary for survival.

TEMPLATES

Your Next Steps

If you're ready to take a systematic approach, here's how to start:

Phase 1: Audit Your Foundation

- **Vision Clarity**: Can everyone in your organization explain in thirty seconds why your company exists and where it's heading?
- **Customer Understanding**: Do you have detailed, evidence-based profiles of your ideal customers and their real motivations?

Phase 2: Assess Your Engine

- **People Alignment**: Are your best people in roles that amplify their strengths? Do you have the right team structures for your current challenges?
- **Organizational Design**: Is your structure built for speed and adaptation, or control and predictability?

Phase 3: Evaluate Your Systems

- **Operating Model**: Are you organized around projects or products? Do you measure activities or outcomes?
- **Decision Making**: Do you make decisions based on assumptions or evidence? Do you design experiments or just implement solutions?

Phase 4: Review Your Execution

- **Strategy Implementation**: What percentage of your strategic initiatives get fully implemented? What's preventing faster, more consistent execution?
- **Technology Strategy**: Is your tech stack amplifying your competitive advantages or constraining them?

The Time Is Now

The window for building systematic competitive advantages is narrowing. As artificial intelligence democratizes many traditional advantages, as global competition intensifies, as customer expectations continue to rise, the companies that will thrive are those that build complete systems rather than optimize individual components.

Your competitors are already working on their next competitive advantage. Some are reading books like this one. Some are implementing these frameworks in their organizations right now.

The question isn't whether you need to build better systems - the market has already decided that for you. The question is whether you'll start building them before or after your competitors gain advantages that become impossible to overcome.

A Personal Note

Building great companies is hard. It requires making difficult decisions with incomplete information. It means accepting you'll fail at some things while you're learning to succeed at others. It demands the humility to admit when something isn't working and the courage to change course.

At the same time, it's also the most rewarding challenge you can take on. When you build a company that consistently creates value for customers, provides meaningful work for employees, and generates returns for shareholders - when you build something that makes the world a little bit better - there's no feeling quite like it.

The frameworks in this book aren't just theories. They're tools that have been tested in the real world by real leaders facing real challenges. They work when you work them consistently and thoughtfully. This will require patience in a fast-moving world. And the level of detail you are willing to spend will determine the success.

Your customers need you to build something great. Your employees are counting on you to create an organization where they can do their best work. Your industry needs leaders who will raise the bar for everyone.

The tools are in your hands. The choice is yours. The time is now.

What will you build?

My Favorite Books

As I love reading really good books, I want to mention some of my favorite ones that inspired me and that helped me during my career. You can find more book recommendation on my web site with a list that will be constantly updated.

> **Measure What Matters by John Doerr**
>
> Best book for understanding and implementing OKRs

> **The 5 Dysfunctions of a Team by Patrick Lencioni**
>
> Great book on how to assemble great teams of diverse personalities

> **$100M OFFERS by Alex Hormozi**
>
> Must read to understand what makes an offer so great that people want to buy

> **Feck Perfuction by James Victore**
>
> I love this book, very inspiring for thinking out of the box

> **RADICAL CANDOR by Sheryl Sandberg**
>
> Essential for communication whether you are leading people or not

www.ingramcontent.com/pod-product-compliance
Lightning Source LLC
LaVergne TN
LVHW010639110826
845149LV00014B/2883

* 9 7 8 3 9 8 2 8 1 0 2 3 2 *